Radical Departures

Radical

Desperate Detours
to Growing Up

Saul V. Levine
M.D.

A Harvest/HBJ Book

Harcourt Brace Jovanovich, Publishers

Departures

San Diego   New York   London

Copyright © 1984 by Saul V. Levine
Introduction copyright © 1984 by Harcourt Brace Jovanovich, Inc.

Library of Congress Cataloging in Publication Data
Levine, Saul V., 1938–
    Radical departures.
    Bibliography: p.
    Includes index.
    1. Cults—Psychological aspects—Case studies.
I. Title.
BL80.2.L46   1984   306'.1   83-26491
ISBN 0-15-175840-9
ISBN 0-15-675799-0 (Harvest/HBJ : pbk.)

Designed by Jacqueline Schuman
Printed in the United States of America
First Harvest/HBJ edition 1986
A B C D E F G H I J

To Ellie, Jaime, Mischa, and Zachary

Contents

Acknowledgments

I'm not sure that I would have undertaken this book had I anticipated just how tyrannical the task was to become. As arduous as the experience was, however, the gratifications transcended the difficulties. Not the least of those gratifications was the realization of how many people stood ready to help with their good will, patience, talent, and energy.

First, and certainly foremost, I am indebted to the hundreds of young people who allowed me to interview them extensively during their radical departure and sometimes to continue to badger them for years after their return. I am grateful too for the cooperation of their parents, who often met with me under trying circumstances, and to the group leaders who graciously facilitated my work.

My earliest studies came to fruition through the help of hard-working collaborators, including Robert Carr, William Longdon, David Lloyd, Wendy Horenblas, and especially Nancy Salter. My thanks and apologies are due to my colleagues at Sunnybrook Medical Centre and the University of Toronto, who tolerated my preoccupation with radical departures, and to Carole Segal, our department manager, who helped me in so many ways during the period of writing.

I am also indebted to Betty Hamburg for general inspiration (although she doesn't know it), to Judy Rasminsky for editorial advice and guidance, to Bernard (Berl) Schiff for his critical reading, to Vivian Rakoff, Quentin Rae-Grant, and Fred Lowy for their encouragement, and to my other friends who put up with my mishugass.

I particularly thank Rose Williams. She not only put up with drudgery, but acceded to deadline demands with patient good cheer all through the task of typing and transmitting manuscript between Toronto and New York. Bonnie Gallay and Regina Erdelyi are also to be thanked for their help with the typing, and Jo Meingarten for her early editorial assistance.

There is also my editor, Sara Bonnett Stein. For her overriding belief in the book, her yeoman effort to clarify my writing, her encouragement when I wanted to pack it in, her ability to lay criticism, and compliments, on the line, and the enormous amount of thought and work she gave to the project, I thank her very much.

Finally, my wife, Ellie, and sons, Jaime, Mischa, and Zachary, deserve my undying gratitude for supporting, cajoling, tolerating, inspiring, and loving me. They are my (not so) radical departure.

Introduction

As I read this exceptionally clearheaded and thoughtful book I remembered a poetry reading of William Carlos Williams in the early 1950s. He was old and sick but still energetic and shrewd as he interrupted himself, stopped singing with passion his own lines, in order to make this brief critical comment: "I struggled hard with these poems; I struggled for a certain balance. With what success? I leave it to you to come up with a verdict!" I believe Dr. Levine wanted very much to do likewise—achieve a certain symmetry, a certain proportion, for his lines of reasoning; and I think he has succeeded splendidly.

The subject matter might easily have made for quite another outcome. This is a book about the irrational if not the weird—and in some instances, the downright loony, even the terribly dangerous: the myriad cults which persist into the mid–nineteen eighties, well after the time of the so-called "youth culture," which flourished two decades ago and was supposed to have died. But the author, a child psychiatrist of long experience, has not allowed himself to become overwhelmed by a given subject matter—stirred to hysteria and fearful self-righteousness. On the contrary, his evident calm, his firm detachment (though at no cost of empathy), are notably reassuring to the reader, who at moments may become anxious for some of the youths whose life stories are rendered and who also may become worried for all of us who share with these young men and women a common time spent on this planet.

I must admit that as I began to meet these young men and women through Dr. Levine's sensitive portraits, I found myself impatient with some of them, or angry at their decision to leave so drastically the ordinary world (middle-class version) so many of us take for granted most of the time and, during our more aware and grateful moments, remember to celebrate. I also felt pangs of urgent sorrow for the parents Dr. Levine mentions—perhaps because I am a father of three sons attending college and high school. Not least, I felt impatience and at moments disgust as I read about some of the cults—the absurdity of their claims, the conniving and corruption of their leaders. Yet Dr. Levine is wonderfully helpful with the reader. He helps one calm down and take a careful, thoughtful look at a given human phenomenon. He offers a broad and deep perspective on what is really happening to the young people who get involved with cults and, just as important, what (mostly) doesn't happen.

We tend to fear (and suspect) the worst—that young and vulnerable lives are irretrievably lost. Such is not the case, Dr. Levine tells us. The overwhelming majority of those who make these various "radical departures," who sign up with one or another marginal group (religious, political, ecological, psychological), will in the long run return to the regular, conventional lives most of us live. Put differently, these "departures" are temporary in nature—and of course made by only a relative handful of youths. Within a year or two there is another "departure," this time away from the Moonies and the Scientologists and God knows what other organization or community of wayward souls.

We expect from Dr. Levine some answers to inevitable questions. We want to know precisely which youths join these "cults" and for what reasons. We want to know what ought be done—for the sake of the given young man or young woman and, of course, for the sake of our society. Most of all, I hope, we reach out for the particular youths—asking ourselves what in their lives prompted such a strenuous "departure." On all these scores, the author is sensible and wise in his answers. He refuses to embrace high-handed theory. He lets us know that there simply aren't the categorical generalizations we crave—that no one psychological statement explains the motives, hopes, worries, ideals, of these youths; that they come from a range of cultural and religious backgrounds, though their middle-class mode of life enables the leap of sorts they take; that there is no sure way to predict either who will, finally, make a "radical departure" or who is likely (a small minority) to stay with a cult more or less indefinitely.

Not that the author hasn't a few pointed observations of a more abstract kind to make—and even a recommendation or two for those readers caught in the turmoil he so well understands through his work of years with parents of young cultists. This book does justice to the complexity of twentieth-century adolescence as it takes place in Western industrial societies among reasonably well-to-do people—the almost desperate search for an independent self undertaken by growing boys and girls who may have unprecedented "creature-comforts" yet who feel, often enough, confused and uncertain and, yes, morally adrift. What to do? Where? How to go about doing it? With whom? As we read Dr. Levine's medical stories or vignettes we begin to learn about the stresses of growing up as experienced by certain individuals, and not by them alone. We also begin to appreciate what some cults offer—a moral certainty that is avowed ceaselessly. When such an offering is combined with the powerful currents set in motion by a group's solidarity, the draw is strong indeed for certain susceptible, if not vulnerable, individuals. As Dr. Levine suggests, we ought ask not only about the "psychopathology" of these youths but about what could have spared them such a radical turn: idealistic possibilities, sanctioned by our society, which might well have made a crucial difference—that is, inspired a less severe renunciation of the conventional world.

Especially valuable is the overall tone of this book—an edifying contrast to the authoritarian character of many cults. Dr. Levine is tactful, considerate, open-minded. He has a novelist's sensibility—is responsive to this life's mysteries, its never-ending ironies and ambiguities, its thickly textured mix of uncertainty, surprise, and accident. He wants us to confront not only certain perplexed and (often enough) frantically apprehensive youths but ourselves—the world we sometimes fail to examine closely enough. These "radical departures" turn out to be, in this doctor's hands, this writer's presentation, an invitation to a look at yet another "them," true, but perhaps more significant, an occasion for self-scrutiny on our part and, one hopes, for a bit of social and moral reflection: what kind of world do we want for our young and how might we proceed, right now, to help make the changes which might bring such a world closer to realization?

Robert Coles
Cambridge, Massachusetts

Radical Departures

1

Facing Facts

June 27, 1983 dawned bright and breezy in the Bay Area. Around the breakfast table in the Thomas home in an affluent suburb, good-humored conversation was interrupted by the honk of a horn. Mark got up from the table, put his plate and cup in the kitchen sink, grabbed the sweater slung over the back of his chair, and made for the door to join his friends.

His father stopped him. Pressing a twenty-dollar bill into Mark's hand, he rested his arm for a moment over his son's shoulder and made an embarrassed joke about the money. "Just in case you guys get into trouble in the big city." He winked.

Mr. Thomas could afford to make such jokes. Mark, as clean-cut a blond as any model middle-class family could hope to produce, had never been in trouble in his life. He wasn't outstanding in any particular way, but he was a willing, smiling, reliable boy, the sort who is chosen to monitor the halls in grade school, who volunteers for community projects in junior high, and, in high school, runs the committee to make arrangements for the senior prom.

The horn honked a second time—they had a train to catch—and, after kissing his mother good-by, Mark strode out the door to the waiting car. It was the Monday after high-school graduation. Mark and his friends were on their way to celebrate: six kids on a lark one sunny day in San Francisco.

When the group returned that evening, Mark wasn't with them. His friends had last seen him late that afternoon in Golden Gate Park, where they had gone together to share a six-pack of beer and watch the sun go down. The Thomases weren't worried. They figured that Mark had simply missed the agreed-upon train. He had that extra twenty "just in case." Since trains run from San Francisco to its suburbs on a commuter schedule, they expected his call from the station shortly.

But the phone didn't ring that night. In the morning, the police were notified.

After seventy-two hours of mounting panic, the Thomases at last heard from Mark. They weren't to worry, he told them during the collect call from Oregon. He was fine. He was more than fine; he was happier than he had ever been in his life. He had joined the Rajneesh Bhagwan. He had made a radical departure.

Every year thousands of young people abruptly turn their backs on family, friends, and their very future to join one or another of an estimated 2,500 communal groups in North America whose values, dress, and behavior seem totally alien and often inimical to everything the joiner has ever stood for.

The Rajneesh Meditation Centers, one of which Mark Thomas joined, are led by Bhagwan Shree Rajneesh, called by members the "Enlightened Master." He owns twenty-eight Rolls-Royces. The group bought 64,000 acres in Oregon in 1980, moved in the following year, and, several hundred strong, took over town government in the small community of Antelope. The town's original population is depleted now; many felt forced to move because of infuriating local legislation they could no longer control.

Followers of the Rajneesh Bhagwan wear colorful clothing of pink, red, burgundy, and orange. Around their necks hang long strands of beads with a large pendant bearing the portrait of their Enlightened

Master. They believe in "dynamic meditation" and "the discipline of non-discipline." When the Thomases next saw their son, he was on a street corner in Portland chanting in a circle dance, dressed in red, hood pulled over his clean-cut blond head. He refused to turn toward his father's call; he showed no sign of even recognizing his parents.

Radical departures like this are a fact of life today, a phenomenon that has inspired more fear, anger, agony, disgust—and misinterpretation—than almost any other. Mark Thomas's departure was only a recent one among many hundreds I have studied since the late 1960s. Those were the days of the Flower Children, Hippies, Yippies, and the rise of the urban commune. "Make love, not war" seemed, to youth at that time, a reasonable answer to the world's problems; the sunny yellow "happy face" was soon to become their special insigne. Kids who only a few years before had had faith in their alma maters barricaded themselves in their college administration buildings, demanded curriculums of their own choosing, broke time-honored rules with abandon, and dropped out in droves. Dropping out also seemed an answer. "Turn on, tune in, drop out," Timothy Leary advised followers, who took the slogan as their rationale for tripping on hallucinogens. For a while everything seemed to break out in the strange colors and patterns of those delusional visions.

It was in this atmosphere of distrust, disillusion, and alienation among young people that the Jews for Jesus, the Hare Krishna, the Moonies, and many other such groups put down their roots. I was then barely beyond my student days, only a few years out of medical school at McGill University, in Montreal, and completing my psychiatric residency at Stanford University Medical Center, in California. These new groups appeared to be hostilely opposed to the backbone standards of middle-class conduct. Beyond that, there was a lot of confusion, especially among people my age—almost thirty and therefore not to be trusted, still approaching thirty and therefore close to the grass roots of youthful discontent. Some of the stands taken seemed right to me— for civil rights, against a futile war—but some of what I saw disturbed me deeply.

My clinical work had already introduced me to a subpopulation of dropouts, really troubled youngsters who lived in filthy drug communes in the Haight-Ashbury and elsewhere in the California counterculture. These youths had, as psychiatry would expect, personal histories of academic failure, social isolation, and chronically embattled home lives as prelude to their dangerous chemical addictions. Based on that limited exposure, it was possible to indict radical commitment in general as a manifestation of pathology.

Most psychiatrists agreed with that judgment. Professional consensus was that joiners had come from sordid backgrounds and were obviously disturbed to have succumbed so impulsively to antisocial movements. Some laymen agreed; others had other explanations. The most charitable view was that those who joined charismatic fringe groups were gullible innocents who had been "brainwashed"—a striking neologism in its peacetime use which seemed to explain the almost magical power a leader might hold over his followers. Some saw group members not as victims at all, but as zealots infused with bigotry and violence aimed at the subversion of traditional values. One thing everyone seemed to agree on was that these were not ordinary, well-brought-up middle-class kids, the ones on "Happy Days" and the ones we ourselves had been or were raising now.

Therefore, I was surprised to find, as my interest in adolescent and young-adult development took me along the underground railway that routed draft dodgers to Canada, that these protesters, massed in urban communes or converted to a variety of intensely ideological group beliefs, during the early 1970s, came right out of "Happy Days."

There was no more sign of pathology among them than is found in any youthful population. These youngsters were from warm, concerned homes, not from a disrupted underclass. Their families were prosperous and had given them every material, social, and intellectual benefit widely believed to ensure happiness and success. They were, in short, like Mark Thomas—good kids from good backgrounds with everything to look forward to. They could be anyone's kids.

What had become of them was something else again. Those who have followed media reports on any of the groups loosely labeled "cults" have been treated to a first impression not very different from what I at first perceived. Such groups, it would seem, are gripped by a charismatic leader who uses his power to enrich and elevate himself unconscionably. The beliefs he perpetrates are counterfeit: travesties at best, sheer malevolence at worst. Those who follow him either are duped to give up their true selves and serve their "master" or are forced to do so against their will. To this end they may be held captive by force, deprived of financial means to make their escape, prevented from communicating with their families, or induced to fear all those whom they formerly loved.

The Children of God have been rumored to censor incoming and outgoing mail and to prevent any privacy by means of an intrusive buddy system. Upon joining, youngsters are required to sign a statement that begins "I promise to give all my goods and income . . ." The very words of the Bible are used to turn children against their parents. "For I am come to set a man at variance against his father, and the daughter against her mother," the group preaches, using a text from Matthew. Members call themselves "revolutionary Christian nomads" and say they are in a "war of the Spirit against the System's Godless schools, Christless churches and heartless Mammon"—a broad category of "Systemites" that manages to include all the rest of us. In order to bring Systemites "to Jesus," inexperienced girls are encouraged to be "happy hookers in Christ." That is, they are sexually to seduce new membership.

The hold a leader can have over his following is shocking. At a Divine Light Mission rally I attended in 1976, 8,000 youngsters were moved to tears of rapture by the fatuous speech of their master, the Maharaj Ji, who used the word "beautiful" twenty-seven times in three and a half minutes. For four hours the following day, 10,000 members lined up to kiss their Perfect Master's feet. To hustle the line along, the master's henchmen literally grabbed each from the midst of obeisance and shoved him or her on to make room for the next. These henchmen were trained in military tactics.

Tactics demanded of members are no less abhorrent in many cases. The Reverend Sun Myung Moon of the Holy Spirit Association for the Unification Church—contracted to Unification Church or simply called "the Moonies"—preaches "Heavenly deception." Members seek donations in airports and other busy public places by selling flowers to benefit a fictional home for the retarded or some other nonexistent cause.

Their tactic is to bar the way of hurried travelers with smiling entreaty, making it clear that it would be easier to reach for some change than to brush them off. While the Unification Church is nominally a Christian organization, Moon's own delusion of omnipotence includes his claim to be the Messiah. Eve, he tells his members, subverted God's plan to create perfect mankind when she was seduced by Lucifer. Moon and his wife, Mrs. Moon, fulfill God's original intent: they are the "perfect parents." The Reverend Moon recently indulged his omnipotence by arranging for the mass marriage of over 4,000 of his membership, which he claims to be 300,000 worldwide.

Rituals bizarre to most tastes are the earmark especially of groups with Oriental pretensions. The Society of Krishna Consciousness draws on Oriental philosophies to come up with the strange amalgam that became familiar to us in the words of the song "My Sweet Lord," by George Harrison of the Beatles. The lyrics include the Hare Krishna chant that repeats the names of the Krishna God in his different manifestations: "Hare Krishna, Hare Krishna, Krishna Krishna, Hare Hare, Hare Rama, Hare Rama, Rama Rama, Hare Hare." Thus chanting, members work themselves into a trancelike state in which they appear totally removed from contact with the outside world. Young male members dress in saffron yellow robes, shave their heads except for a pigtail, and smear a stripe of ash from forehead to nose tip.

Exotic costuming is *de rigueur* also for the Healthy Happy Holy Organization, the first radically alien religious commune I came to know as a result of my clinical practice among draft dodgers. Its members dress in floor-length white robes and wear white turbans. With no overtones of Christianity at all, they practice a demanding form of yoga that requires strict vegetarianism and abstinence from a variety of other indulgences rarely seen as moral issues in middle-class culture.

Sometimes the degree of asceticism practiced by a group is distressing, and leaders have been accused of supplying inadequate nutrition to members or of failing to house and clothe them in a healthy manner. Medical attention is sometimes less than what an affluent family, accustomed to consulting a private practitioner for even routine viral infections such as colds and intestinal illnesses, would want for their child. Some members are so carried away by their faith that, regardless of whether or not the group believes in spiritual cures for physical af-flictions, they may themselves ignore symptoms. Some fundamentalist Jewish groups that attract radical departers eschew luxury to the point of real physical discomfort, and lead a life that offers almost no op-portunity for exercise. A zealous rabbi in one such group considered five hours of sleep a night to be sufficient for members, some of whom were still literally growing.

As I gradually came to be involved in the study of such groups, first in my native Canada and later in the United States, Europe, and Israel, I found that much as these first impressions accorded with me-dia sensationalism, most of the time they did not. The media have used the word "cult" categorically to describe, not only the grotesque excesses that led to the Manson murders in 1969 and the mass suicide by cyanide poisoning of members of the People's Temple in Jones-town, Guyana, in 1978, but also to any group utilized by youngsters for radical departures. The Manson group was openly racist; Jim Jones, leader of the People's Temple, was a dangerous psychotic; there are witchcraft groups that believe in possession by the Devil. I have seen bad things, but in the hundreds of groups I know at first hand, I have not seen excesses worthy of the pejorative "cult." Indeed, no word in use when I was beginning my studies or in use now adequately char-acterizes the groups young people fervently join when they sever themselves from their accustomed pursuits.

Many such groups espouse forms of mysticism that, although un-usual in our society, represent the mainstream values of other soci-eties. I learned that lesson quickly; the Healthy Happy Holy Organization, which I met early, uses techniques of meditation and self-discipline that have stood the test of thousands of years in India. Oriental religions in general make respectable inquiry into the phili-sophical significance of life, and are not to be belittled by epithets. Other religious groups, including fundamentalist Jewish or Christian ones, may lie toward an extreme end of the spectrum of their respec-tive traditions, but they are by no means outside them. However sim-ilar two religious groups may appear to outsiders, each may call the other a cult, though not itself. Such judgments are in the eye of the beholder. Moreover, many of the groups young people utilize for radical departure are not religious at all. One may speak of their cultish ritual or charismatic leadership, but this isn't helpful, and certainly it is inaccurate to call them cults.

The Armed Guard, for example, was a militant political group that preached anarchy. Any social regulation, whether it emanated from powerful capitalists or from middle-class standards, was, members believed, intended to subjugate the masses. Members sported Gucci loafers, but they performed acts of political sabotage, including amateurish bombings, directed always at their own culture, never toward those such as the Soviet Union's that others might consider repressive.

Some other organizations chosen for radical departures claim to have therapeutic answers. They are youth's version of Primal Centers, EST, Esalen, Bioenergetics, Therafields, and other demandingly intense offshoots of the human-potential movement. The Healing Workshop, a small therapeutic commune representative of many that have cropped up, on the West Coast especially, held pillow-smashing sessions in order to "get in touch with and express" members' anger. The Church of Scientology is avowedly opposed to psychiatry in any form, yet has adopted and distorted psychiatric concepts. For instance, it uses a crude lie detector—a homemade galvanometer it calls an "E-meter"—which it claims gets rid of "conflicted memory traces" so that members can become "clear" of "engrams," or early childhood conflicts. The procedure costs members up to $10,000, making this worldwide organization of 2 to 3 million members among the wealthiest of such groups. It boasted an annual income of $70 million in the United States alone during the mid-1970s.

Because the groups that young people like Mark Thomas are drawn to lend themselves to existing terminology—and certainly are not all cults—I have had to resort to the term "radical" to describe both the groups and the joiners who make them possible. The word "radical" to describe a group, its members, and the act of their departure from their usual lives must be understood as a relative term. There are segments of society who would not see born-again fundamentalism as radical, or who would be able to accept extreme rightist or leftist ideologies, or to whom even the most peculiar therapies would seem reasonable. Throughout this book I will speak of *radical groups, radical departures*, and *radical departers* because, to the families of joiners, the beliefs and behavior of their sons and daughters strike them as radically opposed to their own intellectual, spiritual, and social standards.

Although there is an underlying structure that makes all these groups similar to one another despite the variety of their outer forms—and that structure does have to do with the fantasied omniscience of leaders, rigid belief systems opposed to the outside world, and a studied "strangeness" that is equally hostile—the earmark of a radical departure is less the specifics of the group joined than the rapid transformation of the joiner.

Mark Thomas could not say when, if ever, he would return from the Rajneesh center. His previous plans for entering college the coming fall no longer meant a thing to him. This is unlike other youthful leave-takings—planned intermissions that are responsible or irresponsible, but are limited by time and circumstance. The commitment these young men and women feel is, as far as they know, for the rest of their lives.

The sudden sense of meaninglessness that obviates plans for education or career also obliterates any other interests the joiner previously had. Voracious readers stop reading anything except the tracts provided within their group. Those who had shown talent in music and had always faithfully practiced their instruments no longer care. Athletes stop exercising; nature lovers turn their backs on woods and meadows; artists stop sketching. There is an ominous narrowing of horizons, until only a slit of absolute believing represents the totality of their intellectual pursuit.

Yet even this is not intellectual. Anything recognizable as inquiry, challenge, or analysis comes to an immediate halt. Whatever the belief system of the group is, it seems to the new member to hold the Answer in a form so self-evident and so transcendent that he need only accept it utterly. The Answer is embodied in the group leader, whom the member quite simply adores. In contrast, those outside the group are ridiculed, disdained, and frequently feared.

That includes parents. When Mark Thomas kissed his mother goodby, the gesture proved to have a finality that seems incomprehensible. Between that kiss and the telephone conversation from Oregon seventy-two hours later, this pleasing child came to reject, not only every over-ture of love, but also the opinions, values, ethics, and behavior of his mother and father, all their relatives, all former friends, teachers, and anybody not among the Rajneesh followers. Capitulation to the group is complete; hostility to outsiders is equally so. Within one week, Mark became a stranger.

And these strangers are strange. Personality becomes as shriveled as does intellect. There is a programed quality to their discourse, whether it is being used in defense of their newfound beliefs or in attack on others' longstanding ones. They parrot their leader without being able to come up with phrasing or intonation, not to mention argument, unique to themselves. Eerier still, their delivery is jarringly euphoric. Mark, both over the telephone and when the Thomases attempted to break through to him on the street corner in Portland, was in a smil-ing state of bliss, so concentrated on feelings of love that he could not be distracted by his father's voice or either parent's unhappy expres-sion. It is a cruel happiness, one must conclude, that can be so re-jecting of others.

This sudden transformation of a child known intimately within the family for almost two decades is an ultimate horror. The dimpled baby the parents once knew now rants a sort of gibberish that is less com-municative by far than the goos and aahs of infancy. The charming, courageous toddler who once delighted them now retires from chal-lenge and sees every enticement in the outside world as sinful or dan-gerous. Kids in pigtails who pounded the piano and baseball-capped ten-year-olds who went off on camping trips now talk of bombs and bliss with monstrous blandness and uncontagious smiles. "Radical" is not even an extreme enough word to describe the extent of these de-partures. Yet they have never been expected.

I have worked among and with these radical departers and their families since 1969; joiners I have known at least casually number in the thousands. In no case was the sudden leave-taking expected by those who knew the youngster best. These departures are called "out of character" by observers and make no sense to them. Indeed, radical departers, despite the fact that they showed no underlying pathology in the years before their joining, appear to have taken leave of their senses.

In the fifteen years since I followed the first wave of "peaceniks" to Canada, I have learned just how much sense radical departures make. They are desperate attempts to grow up in a society that places obstacles in the way of the normal yearnings of youth. The strangeness that unnerves adults, the hostility that enrages them, and even the euphoria they can't share are expressions of belief and belonging—and of their opposites, disillusion and alienation—that these sons and daughters utilize to support their growing up. Parents suffer from their leave-taking and so do they, but they are trying to do what is expected of them.

In the course of these years of study I have developed what seems to me a workable methodology that balances the need for objective data with no less important subjective impressions. I first meet with the local leader of a group to obtain permission to study his membership. I make clear that my purpose is to understand, not to pass judgment on the group's beliefs or activities. There is no hidden agenda the group need fear. I promise, and have always kept that promise, to share fully the results of my study, though not, of course, privileged information of a personal nature confided by individuals.

Individual participation is voluntary. Sometimes the leader or a senior member will announce the study at an open meeting of the entire membership, explaining that I will be in and out of their group home, office, or temple over the next several months and would welcome individual members who might want to speak with me. Other times the study is publicized by a notice on a bulletin board or informally communicated. In spite of the fact that almost every group deeply suspects the motives of therapists in general—some have been secretive terrorist groups fearful of the law as well—no leader has ever turned down my request, nor has there ever been a lack of volunteers willing to cooperate with me.

For background and in order to familiarize myself with the terminology a group uses, I read the literature that embodies its belief system and attend lectures, rituals, prayers, meetings, and mass rallies as an observer. Some of my studies have been conducted with the help of specialists in other fields, such as urban anthropology or pediatrics, and these differing perspectives have been valuable.

To qualify for participation, members must have been in the group for at least six months. This criterion has been successful in screening out members who are less than fully committed or who are exploiting the group for temporary shelter. The number of interviews is left open. I have been able to meet with most volunteers during the height of their commitment, as their intensity and single-mindedness begins to give way to doubt, and within the first six months of their return home. I have been able to keep track of the whereabouts of many and to do brief follow-ups varying numbers of years after they left the group.

For every member who volunteers I first make a demographic profile: age, education, residence, parents' occupations and marital status, siblings, prior religious training, previous interests. The interview proper starts with rather formal questions that usually elicit pat answers as to why they joined this group, what they feel to be significant about their activities there, and how they feel physically and emotionally at present. As members begin to feel more comfortable with me, I can usually probe for their feelings in the months before their departure, how they are getting on now with their parents, and the relationships they are enjoying within the group. Subsequent meetings explore similar territory concerning later phases of membership and their return from the radical departure. Altogether, there are about five hours of conversation with each volunteer over the span of the study and its follow-up.

During the earliest studies I also made use of several standard psychological inventories, in order to check my own impressions of members' mental health. I no longer do so, for two reasons: there was no discrepancy between test results and my assessment arrived at through interview alone, and psychological testing was considered so nefarious that it interfered with a trusting relationship.

With participants' permission, I also interview their families. Since my interest in radical groups takes me all over North America and to Europe and Israel as well, I have been able to visit hundreds of parents in their homes. When possible, I spend some time with other relatives and with peers who were close friends of the joiner before the radical departure.

Using this technique, I have thoroughly studied a total of fifteen radical groups, ranging from the drug cults of the 1960s and the urban communes of the early 1970s to the religious, political, and therapeutic groups most active today; I have only somewhat less complete knowledge of another ten. Total members interviewed is over 800. In addition, I work clinically with parents and former members outside the study groups. This has given me the chance to know quite intimately the suffering that families endure while their children are in the group, the ways in which mothers and fathers come to some rapprochement with their children, and the cruel task that awaits joiners upon their return.

In addition to this funded research, I have informally followed the activities and learned the character of many dozens of other intensely ideological groups, all of which share some traits with the ones I use as examples in this book, but many of which are not germane to the youth discussed here.

For example, there are scores of fundamentalist, mystic, political, and therapeutic groups that are used as psychological havens or modes of self-expression by adults. Membership in such groups rarely extends downward to the adolescents and young adults who make radical departures. Also, they seldom offer the "home away from home" financially dependent youngsters require; adult members ordinarily remain in their own homes and pursue their usual occupations except for time spent at meetings and retreats. I do want to make clear, however, that any intensely ideological group *may* be used as a radical departure by a young man or woman, a possibility that will become clear in the exploration of the psychological meaning of these leave-takings. Radical departures are distinguished by their symptomatology, not by the superficial nature of the group joined.

Drug groups and urban communes are not included for two reasons. First, both types of groups have nearly vanished from the social scene in the 1980s. Second, both differed fundamentally from groups young people choose for radical departure. Drug groups drew their membership from a chronically disrupted population, whose members, drug dependent or addicted as they were, were unable to use group membership productively. Indeed, such groups were never more than transient fallings-together of troubled people who lacked the practical and social skills necessary to hold the group together. The same transience marked urban communes, although for different reasons. While commune members were loosely tied to one another by virtue of their "liberation" and their need for sharing practical matters of everyday living, they never exhibited the intense ideological devotion and absolute belief that typify radical departers. Members maintained their individuality and their inner freedom to come and go as circumstances required.

To list existing groups that are presently used for radical departure would not be helpful. The nature of groups can change rapidly. An accepted organization such as Synanon, once respected for its drug-treatment centers, was transformed into an exploitive and cultish group, and, research would show, some matured groups, well integrated into society now, had their beginning in radical departure. Those that don't mature tend to be transient. Small groups may dissolve within a couple of years, or less. Even large groups may wax and wane over little more than a decade. And if the many thousands of radical groups I might list today were to disappear off the face of the earth tomorrow, one could take no comfort. New groups would sprout like dandelions in the spring to take their place. It's the phenomenon of radical departure that shows permanence, and not the individual groups that serve it.

Of the nine groups used here to illustrate radical departures in general—already introduced in some of their more upsetting or antisocial aspects—some are real groups with a long history in North America, and some, given fictional names, are amalgams of types of groups that come and go over a period of a decade or less. The Unification Church was founded in South Korea in 1954 and has been centered in the United States since 1969, the same year in which the Children of God was founded in North America. The Armed Guard, not its actual name, exemplifies small and rather loosely organized militant political-activist groups, most of which are short-lived. The Healing Workshop, also a fictional name, represents a type of therapeutic group that might easily join the ranks of those that are today beginning to rival fundamentalism in membership, wealth, and appeal to a vulnerable population.

The vulnerability of adolescents and young adults to radical departure has not diminished since youth experienced the deeply unsettling cynicism of the 1960s. Recently I received a call from terrified parents whose daughter had joined the Jews for Jesus; next week, next month, there will be other calls, other frantic parents, new groups I've never heard of, children lost to years of what should have been their uneventful and gratifying growth to adulthood. Who are these children? Why do they join? What becomes of them?

I will try to answer these questions in that order by looking at nine joiners, first in the months just prior to their departure, then at the moment when they were approached by the group they would join, through the screening process by which they and the group decided to link destinies, and on into the group itself during the period of the joiner's commitment. This historic approach will allow readers to grasp the dynamics of what is happening, for, while the Moonies smilingly offer their deceptive bouquets, the Armed Guard plots the downfall of the way of life in which its members were raised, and the Healing Workshop smashes pillows with puerile self-involvement, something much more likable—indeed, fine and worthy of respect—occurs internally.

This approach is the only way one can come to understand the remarkable endings to these stories of radical departures. Over ninety percent of these leave-takings end in a return home within two years. Virtually all joiners eventually leave their groups. Most important, they are able to resume the sorts of lives their parents had hoped for them and to find gratification and significance in the middle-class world they had totally abjured. In short, they are able to use their radical departure in the service of growing up.

Reassuring as the facts are, they leave a final and disturbing question unanswered. Isn't there a better way? A radical departure is a desperate measure taken by children suffering from a painful developmental stalemate. The agony parents experience is beyond measure. There is damage to society itself: in millions of dollars bilked from members and the public or withheld through spurious tax exemptions, in political and social disruption, in the unease these groups inspire, and, finally, in the uncounted years of concrete progress and giving relationships lost to young people during their commitment.

I hope that the knowledge I have gained and the consideration I have given to a widespread dilemma will help parents to find ways to offer their children helpful, productive, and genuinely benevolent means of surmounting obstacles they have unknowingly placed before them.

2
The Joiners

Dennis Ericson's radical departure was among the first I came to know about. In 1969, when I was working among draft dodgers and deserters in Toronto and other cities in Canada, Dennis was a 20-year-old sophomore studying engineering at the University of Cincinnati. He had no trouble with technical courses, but had to work hard to maintain his grades in the required dose of literature and history. Dennis's stocky figure and sandy hair, cropped short even in those long-haired days, resembled those of his father, Jack. Mr. Ericson had worked as a design engineer since his retirement, as a colonel, from the U.S. Army. Ivy Ericson worked as a loan adviser in a bank. An older brother had already graduated with a degree in engineering, and it was a family joke that one day the three men would hoist a sign: Ericson & Sons, Engineers.

The family lived in a pleasant suburb of San Diego. In keeping with their traditionally conservative professions and with their middle-class, Protestant backgrounds, they supported President Nixon and the Vietnam War effort wholeheartedly. Like other students of his day,

Dennis anticipated being drafted to serve in Vietnam, and he and his family seemed to be in fundamental agreement that serving one's country was not only an obligation, but also a correct and honorable one.

Dennis had no tolerance for antiwar groups such as Students for a Democratic Society and the Student Nonviolent Coordinating Committee; he had considered joining the Young Republicans.

This seamless agreement in principle showed a slightly frayed edge in practice. Dennis on several occasions confided to his parents a certain eagerness to be drafted, and was surprised to find his urge met with nervous amusement. The Ericsons supported the war but didn't want their son to serve in Vietnam.

Dennis had not, however, confided the full extent of his concerns or the underlying reasons for his urge to join the army. Raised in a career-oriented home and enrolled in a career-oriented course of study, he was nevertheless becoming increasingly unsure of the direction in which he was headed. He was bored with his friends, his activities, his studies, himself. Talking about the months just prior to receiving his draft notice, he said, "All I knew then was that I needed some excitement or adventure in my life. I could get into terrific arguments on campus about the war, but for me it was all a mental game. I wished that I believed what I said." Joining up, he felt, might relieve his overwhelming sense of tedium.

When the draft notice did arrive, Dennis abruptly, to his own and his family's confusion, changed his mind. He joined other draft dodgers in a commune in Vancouver. Within weeks he had left this group to become a member of Healthy Happy Holy Organization, usually called "3HO." This spiritual-rehabilitation group followed Yogi Bhajan, an Indian teacher of Tantric and Kundalini Yoga in the United States and Canada.

Philip Holtzman at 21 was the success story all parents wish for their children. He was an excellent student, a star athlete, and popular with both boys and girls; he had a steady girl, Marcie, with whom he was quite taken. During the summer of 1978 this tall boy with tightly curling red hair was living at home in Denver after completing his sophomore year at the University of Colorado. He had taken a variety of arts and science courses, had made the dean's list both years, but felt unready to declare a major. Hoping to come upon some one thing that interested him particularly, he planned to take a year's leave of absence from school to travel and work abroad, and his parents, Sam and Ellen, encouraged the idea. They had no doubt that their older son could take on this new venture with the same responsibility he had always shown; to them, this challenging year was to be an extension of his education.

Education was a central value to the Holtzmans. Sam was a prominent physician. Ellen was a high-school librarian studying for her doctorate in library science. Phil's two younger brothers and a sister were all doing well in school, though not quite at the level of their older brother. Like Phil, his parents were what one would call "well-rounded" people. They regularly attended the local symphony and the theater, and found time for tennis and jogging.

Dr. Holtzman had been brought up in an Orthodox Jewish home in New York City; Yiddish was his parents' native tongue. Mrs. Holtzman came from a Conservative, quite devout Jewish background. Although neither grew up to be deeply religious, they felt strongly about their commitment to Judaism and to Israel. They attended Sabbath services at a Reform temple sporadically, never missed the High Holy Day services, and had seen to it that all of their children received religious training and read some Hebrew.

This "ideal" family was further flavored with idealism. In their own words, they had always encouraged their children to "make a contribution," to "leave the world better than they found it." Their only tension with Phil stemmed from the fact that he had been unable to translate this idealism within the context of their religion. As Phil put it, "I never felt much identification with Judaism or Israel. Mom and Dad got annoyed whenever I spoke this way, but I couldn't help it. Actually, I felt that this was the only area in which I disappointed them. I knew I was Jewish, but I didn't feel much else about it."

That summer, abroad, this model youth made his radical departure into the mysticism and narrow intellectualism of an Orthodox Jewish seminary, a yeshiva in Jerusalem.

Jennifer Green was a 19-year-old beauty. She wore her glistening black hair tied back simply from her perfectly oval, creamy-complexioned face. Her gray eyes sparkled with laughter—"bubbly" laughter, as her mother described it. Jennifer showed the sort of native talent that is peculiarly gratifying to parents. She was a gifted pianist, and the Greens took justifiable pride in their expectation that she would go on to a career as a concert pianist.

The whole family had participated in her talent, even to the extent of moving from their home in the Midwest to Houston, where a sought-after teacher had consented to supervise her training. By the winter after her graduation from high school in 1972, their efforts seemed about to pay off: Jennifer had auditioned for and been accepted by two conservatories, Curtis and Juilliard.

The Greens, however, showed signs of family strain. Allen Green, an accountant and tax consultant employed by a well-heeled clientele, was a busy man whose recipe for getting along with his wife and daughter was to lie low. Linda Green was preoccupied with a campaign to achieve "self-realization"—an endeavor that had led her to espouse at various times Gestalt, Rolfing, Esalen, Bioenergetics, and other therapeutic schemes. Jennifer's older brother, Jason, was completing his doctoral thesis in behavioral modification. Indeed, this faith, for that was what their fervor for therapy seemed to amount to, was practiced by everyone in the family except Mr. Green. From the time Jennifer was 15, Mrs. Green had been convinced that her beautiful, talented daughter needed professional help; and it was true that Jennifer, for all her appeal to her schoolmates, had tended to isolate herself from other children her age. At her mother's behest, she was in group, family, or individual therapy for the next four years, while Mrs. Green harped on the refrain "Develop yourself."

But Jennifer seemed to lose the strands of whatever self she was supposed to be developing. By the time she was accepted by a conservatory, she was only going through the motions in her music; she could work at it, but took no pleasure in practice. Her mother was too adamant to notice. As Jennifer explained, about this period prior to her departure, "My mother was on a tear all the time about my career and the latest guru who would cure my woes."

Jennifer found her "guru" on her own through an ad in a psychology magazine: Kurt, the charismatic leader of the Healing Workshop, a therapeutic commune and another variety of radical departure.

Suzanne Marquette, 18 in 1975, lived with her family in Minneapolis, where she had completed a year of junior college, though with little interest and declining grades. This, and the fact that this pretty, diminutive blond had never had a boyfriend and didn't participate in the active social life her friends enjoyed, might have concerned her parents were it not for the special circumstances of their daughter's life. Suzanne had one overriding passion: figure skating. She was extremely talented and had since the age of five devoted thousands of hours to what she considered one of the higher art forms.

Her mother, Barbara, was deeply involved in that pursuit, chaperoning her daughter to practice, shows, and competitions and always being extremely supportive of her continuing progress. Peter Marquette, Suzanne's father, was perhaps too distracted by his own pursuits to contribute to those of his daughter. He owned a small but thriving printing business, and evidently had to be there morning, noon, and night—the sort of driven man one would call a "workaholic."

Suzanne also had that air of constant busyness. She did everything with a competence and thoroughness unusual in a girl that age. Besides the demands of skating, she did volunteer work at a nursing home and was very helpful around the house. She was particularly tender with her tow-headed twin brothers, whom, though they were only four, she coaxed along on the ice until they were really quite good skaters. "Maybe I was too busy in those days," Suzanne was to tell me later. "I don't know—when I wasn't helping out around the house or at the nursing home, I knew that I had to be skating. And it didn't feel like a burden; I mean I had done that most of my life, and that was just the way things were."

Ice-skating had, indeed, become a career choice as well as a recreation. Suzanne planned to turn professional during the coming fall, when she was scheduled to try out for a well-known ice show in Santa Monica, California. Acceptance into the troupe would mean going on tour. "I was busy but I wasn't involved in things," she explained. "For some reason I knew I couldn't wait to get away on tour, even though I was getting tired of skating."

Lying on the beach in Santa Monica the day of the audition, Suzanne was approached by members of the Unification Church. Sometime in the next three days, and after a most successful audition, she had thrown the years of practice to the wind. She had become a Moonie.

Other young men and women who shocked family and friends with their radical departures were more troublesome to their parents than Dennis, Phil, Jennifer, and Suzanne were.

Nancy Lewis was in constant conflict with her parents over her choice of career and her behavior in general. Her parents had wanted her to go to a small business college not far from their home in northern New Jersey to learn a marketable skill. Nancy, with some contempt for her father's job as a rug salesman, was convinced he saw everything as marketable, even her. She had complied with their wish for one term, then dropped out in favor of informal drama classes run by a New York City actor her father labeled "a loser." Her mother seemed no less crass to Nancy. Mrs. Lewis often remarked on how hard they had worked, how much they had earned, to make her life a happy one.

Nancy's perceptions were not entirely wrong; her parents were not sophisticated and were too often preoccupied with maintaining their middle-class standard of life. The Lewises were nominally Methodist and had sent their three daughters—Nancy was the middle one—to Sunday school, but they themselves rarely attended church. They had few cultural interests. Although their split-level development house was scrupulously cared for, it did not reflect Nancy's idea of creative expression. Mrs. Lewis shopped for supermarket specials on Saturdays; Mr. Lewis watched the ball game and worked around the house on Sundays. All through the week both parents worked hard but unimaginatively to maintain the financial and household standards that, to both of them, stood between them and the much poorer backgrounds both had come from. They were rightly proud of their achievement, but Nancy found their ordinariness dreary. Lillian and George Lewis resented Nancy's apparent ungratefulness.

Nancy responded with what she later called her "grande artiste" front—the belief that she, unlike her parents, was creative, sensitive, cultured. She escaped her house as often as possible to hang out with the guys at "the Elm," smoke a few joints, spend the night with a boyfriend her parents called "a no-good bum," or pick up someone new. She thought these people at least appreciated her creativity, but in fact she was locally known as an "easy lay," which she perhaps inadvertently advertised with overdramatic costuming that accentuated her full breasts and hips.

This desultory sort of life continued for three years without Nancy getting a job, moving away from home, or, as far as the Lewises could see, getting any closer to an acting career. In the winter of 1976, now 22 years old, Nancy looked forward to some relief from the stresses of home life in the form of a two-week vacation in Fort Lauderdale with her close friend, Flo. There she met and joined the Children of God, her radical departure.

Equally bitter but less comprehensible and certainly less likable was Fred Vitelli, a smug young man who by the age of 20 had long since decided that school was "bullshit" and those who remained there "browners." He spoke of others, all others, with contempt weighted with obscenity. If one could ignore his manner, Fred was otherwise attractive: over six feet tall, well built, and with sensual features.

He spent much of his time high or stoned on drugs. He had been suspended from public high school in a wealthy Chicago suburb on two occasions. He had completed secondary education at a private school that specialized in "problem" children, but had refused to apply for college. He had also been in chronic, if minor, trouble with the law—possession of marijuana, reckless driving. Mr. Vitelli, at his wife's pleading for the "baby" in this large family, always bailed Fred out of trouble.

Anthony and Maria Vitelli were one of those couples who by working together in what was originally a small family business—making trophies and commemorative plaques—built their enterprise into a major national concern. They were able to give Fred a Porsche when he was only 17, with the conditional message that the gift was proof of their love but would be taken from him unless he stopped abusing drugs and improved his schoolwork. Fred didn't keep his end of the bargain, but before the Vitellis could reclaim the costly sports car Fred had totaled it. His driver's license was revoked.

By the fall of 1979, parents and son had made another deal. Fred was to go to Europe for a few months, using his own money (which was in fact an accumulation of cash gifts from relatives, not earnings), on condition that he begin college when he returned. Brazen and cocksure on the surface, he intended to spend the forthcoming months stoned, then return to "make a killing" in his family's or some other business. His parents were worn out by this son, unwilling to take him into their business, uncertain of what else to do, yet hopeful that three months on his own would give him the maturity he lacked.

Fred didn't return. In Rome one autumn day he found his radical departure: a militant leftist group of anarchists who called themselves the Armed Guard.

Jamie Gould, 26 years old, was the oldest of the radical departers in this representative sample. His father, John, had made millions as a stockbroker and then moved with his wife to the Bahamas, a location they saw as combination tax haven, retirement home, and center for wheeling and dealing. After a long marriage, they had separated just before Jamie's birthday that year of 1977, and Joanne Gould had begun to divide her time between her own house on Barbados and a villa on the Riviera both provided by her husband. Jamie expected a trust fund worth $4 million when he turned 30. While awaiting this largesse he was free to use the substantial income from the trust as he wished, and he also received a monthly allowance from his father that was expressly to support a lavish brownstone house in New York City.

After graduating from Northwestern University with an arts degree and being accepted into law school, Jamie had turned his back on education. This brief flirtation with becoming a lawyer was one example of his lifelong pattern of transient enthusiasms followed by inertia. The pattern was not unlike that of Mrs. Gould, who suffered from endless fits and starts—collecting Chinese porcelain, sponsoring a local histor-

ical society, organizing through her church a drive to aid famine victims, participating in political demonstrations, raising Persian cats.
People had often remarked that Jamie and his mother looked alike,
with their almost mahogany hair and precisely chiseled features.

Between bouts of optimism, Jamie's aimlessness was crushing. He
had no job and no longstanding interests; a girl who lived with him in
the luxury of his brownstone was seen as a sexual convenience.

Jamie's parents called him regularly, using a three-way connection, a "conference call," but conversation was largely perfunctory. The
Goulds' main concern, or so it appeared to Jamie, was that he wore
an earring in one ear. Their hesitancy about criticizing him any more
deeply than that was in contrast to the outspokenness of their older
son, John Jr., who had become a lawyer. John Jr. was furious at Jamie's total apathy, but his anger didn't really bother Jamie. "I just felt
that my brother was a pain. If he wanted to work so hard that was his
business, but I felt that I had the bread, why not enjoy it?"

Neither Jamie nor his parents seemed able to overcome the physical and emotional distance from which their cash currency of love
was disbursed. "In a strange way," Jamie told me, "I think that money
paralyzed me"—until he joined the Church of Scientology, a quasi-
religion, quasi-psychology which follows the bizarre teachings of L. Ron
Hubbard.

Kathy O'Connor, unlike Jamie, had been very close to her family, until the age of 23. Although she lived in Montreal and they lived in a
rural area some miles north of the city, she had visited them often.
She was a senior nurse at a university medical center, and was described by those who knew this five-foot-five freckle-faced young woman
as "warm," "cheerful," "energetic," and "humane." Fellow nurses especially used the word "wholesome" to sum up Kathy's personality.

The O'Connor family itself might have been described that way.
Katherine O'Connor was a bustling, brisk woman who not only had
cared for her four daughters with unflappable good cheer, but also had
seemed to feed the whole neighborhood's kids while they were growing
up. She was always involved in this or that minor crisis among her

numerous relatives. Her personal dedication to Catholicism was equally cheerful; she believed that it held all the instructions for managing whatever life might deliver.

Charles O'Connor was a public-works administrator for the Montreal city government, and donated time and effort as a scoutmaster. Charles and Katherine were well satisfied that they had devoted their lives to charity, one in the public sphere, the other in service to the family.

But Kathy's relationship with her parents had taken a nose dive the year, 1970, she fell in love with Michael, a young Protestant intern at her hospital. Kathy and Michael both called what had happened between them "love at first sight"; their love was exuberantly sexual. The O'Connors were unable to accept the blatant way in which the two lovers made clear that they were living together. Their three other daughters, one younger and two older than Kathy, were already married, within their faith, to men of whom the family wholeheartedly approved. They could foresee nothing but problems in a mixed marriage, and blamed what was to them their daughter's sinful behavior on her straying from her faith.

Kathy said to me in retrospect, "They wanted what was best for me. It's true they didn't like Michael's religion, but they also resented his liberal politics. I was happy to leave Montreal after our wedding."

The newly married couple moved to New Orleans, where Michael entered an arduous residency in surgery. Kathy saw little of her husband during those months; she couldn't find a senior nursing position; the other residents' wives struck her as shallow people.

After less than half a year of marriage, Kathy left her husband and career to join the Maharaj Ji and his Divine Light Mission.

I was struck by Ethan Browning's intensity when I first met him. He wasn't particularly handsome, though his slight, tanned body emitted energy and his wide hazel eyes were appealing. He was shy, or perhaps reserved is a better way to describe him, for he had learned his manners so well that little spontaneity came through. He used a vocabulary astonishing in one so young.

Ethan, at 16, was the youngest of the joiners in this sample. He was the only child of Stuart Browning, a vice president of a major oil company, and his wife, Patricia, who devoted herself to Ethan's upbringing and to Episcopal church activities. Ethan was in the tenth grade at a special high school for gifted students. Rather a loner, he had only one close friend, also a restrained, bookish boy.

Quiet as he was, Ethan did engage in activities that others saw as social. He was the top chess player in his school and regularly participated in competitions. He was an avid and skilled sailor, both solo and as crew in races. A flutist as well, he was given most of the solo parts in the school ensemble to which he belonged. While he did extremely well in school, he learned so easily that he didn't need to devote a great deal of time to his studies. In his ample spare time, he read voraciously, several books at a time, in subjects as diverse as history, science, and philosophy.

The Browning household was comfortable, if somewhat austere. The year before Ethan's departure in 1976 the family had sold their large home in the suburbs and purchased a well-appointed town house in Boston from which they could walk to work, school, and church. They felt that with Ethan so uninvolved with the suburban life style, they could easily live in the city. Mealtime at the Brownings was polite, a time of well-regulated conversation on a variety of intellectual topics. It held a special place within the family's ordered routine, especially for Ethan, perhaps the most orderly of all, who particularly enjoyed formal debate with his father over dinner.

Ethan never participated, however, in his parents' Episcopal church activities, not even accompanying them to Sunday services. He had said for years that he was an atheist. This bothered the Brownings. Ethan could be obstinately opinionated, and though his parents recognized obstinacy as almost a family trademark, this particular expression of it made them uncomfortable. Their church was central to their lives.

"I knew that at the age of 16, I wasn't a happy person," Ethan confided to me later. "I wasn't suicidal or even depressed, but I felt that something was missing from my life. I learned so much and did so well, yet nothing contented me. I felt there had to be more to my life."

Ethan found what was missing in his radical departure into the Hare Krishna.

Different as these joiners were in personality, talent, and interests, there are similarities among them. Whereas a person who succumbs to a radical departure is as likely to be a girl as a boy, she or he is not likely to be younger than Ethan Browning, 16, or older than Jamie Gould, 26. Those few years from adolescence to early adulthood are about the only time in our society when people *can* depart. Younger than 16 they are too dependent on their families, both emotionally and economically. Older than 26 they are likely to have responsibilities of their own—jobs, families—that they cannot easily abandon.

For a similar reason, radical departures are made almost exclusively by as yet unmarried youngsters from the middle or upper middle class, or from among the decidedly rich. Less affluent young people have neither the luxury nor the leisure to depart from obligations; they must pay their own way and often help their families too. Those who make radical departures do not have to pay their own way, nor do their families rely on support from their children. Jennifer Green's family even paid for her membership in the Healing Workshop, as Phil Holtzman's family paid for his year abroad and Suzanne Marquette's family supported her skating.

Thus, although I have seen one boy as young as 14 and occasional joiners in their 30s, radical departures are, with few exceptions, a phenomenon of late adolescence and early adulthood—the only time when there is the luxury and the leisure suddenly to drop out of usual pursuits.

Because of their age and economic situation, the vast majority of these young people are well educated; most are in their college years when they make their decision to leave their traditional paths. Almost all are white. The connection between race and radical departure is indirect, partly because of the underrepresentation of other groups in the middle class, and partly a result of the fact that joiners look especially for groups made up of members almost exactly like themselves.

Cults such as the People's Temple, which was made up of adults and entire families, most of them black, rarely attract those youths who make radical departures. Indeed, such groups are themselves a rarity; adults who look for impassioned causes or religions seldom depart from other responsibilities in order to satisfy their need, nor do they ordinarily leave home to live communally. That these young people do leave home is all the more extraordinary in that almost all of them come from intact families. Reviews of all the statistics that have been gathered about radical departures indicate that the divorce rate in joiners' families is considerably below the national rate.

But these are constraints on who *can* become a radical departer, and not an explanation of who *chooses* to depart. Obviously, few of all those affluent youths who might give up education, career, family, and friendships to immerse themselves in the Hare Krishna, the Children of God, the Armed Guard, or the Healing Workshop do so. To understand what it is about them that is different from their contemporaries who struggle on in the larger society, it is necessary to take a look at what is happening internally during the decade from 16 years old to 26.

The school years up to about the age of 12 are ordinarily a time of quite smooth progress. By his birthday each year, a child had grown an inch or so taller, reads at a grade level higher than the year before, and conducts himself with measurably greater sophistication. In the following six years, adolescents may grow five inches between one birthday and the next. Their bodies change shape so radically and rapidly that they have to look at themselves in the mirror constantly to see who they are and how they like it. They may leap in a single bound from reading Judy Blume to enjoying Dostoevsky. And as far as behavior is concerned, parents, and they themselves, hardly know what to expect from hour to hour, much less from month to month.

These physical, emotional, and intellectual changes are biological in nature, a result of built-in programs of maturation over which children have no control. Nature dumps on them, so to speak, the makings of adulthood but doesn't necessarily tell them what to make of it. That's the job of society, the nexus where nature and nurture meet to produce what each culture considers to be the best way to realize the potential of the next generation.

Middle-class culture strongly believes that to be a successful adult, a child must during these years separate from his family and establish his individualism from both a practical and a psychological stand-point.

Teen-agers have long since come partway along this road to auton-omy. Infants, as far as can be told, have no clear sense that their in-ternal world is distinct from the external world, so that their wishing for milk and their mother providing milk arise from a union that en-compasses both of them. As babies become able to get some distance from their mother—literal physical distance as they learn to crawl and emotional distance as they discover that their wish and her fulfillment aren't always in accord—they begin to construct a self-awareness sep-arate from that of their parents.

By toddlerhood what they are up to can clearly be seen. Toddlers test out all sorts of distinctions between themselves and others—who wants to wear what, eat what, touch what, and go to bed when—that will serve as markers of their separate estate. Realistically though, pre-schoolers know themselves to be dependent on parents and wisely don't push their differences too far. Indeed, they look out for their own safety by establishing bonds with their parents in the form of identifications ("Don't I look like Mommy?") and behaviors that their parents will love them for ("I'm a good boy!"). When by the age of 5 or 6 the bonds are safely tied, and yet the child has sufficient distance to enjoy a modicum of self-reliance, a time of peace descends. There is per-haps no nicer time within a family than when the children are all of school age but not yet into the upheavals of adolescence.

When the latter stage is reached, the maneuvers to see who's who resume. By then, the child is working from a position of much greater strength. He has self-care skills: selecting clothes, earning money, pur-suing interests independently, and regulating his own life through the whole panoply of negotiations that have, over the years, replaced mere infantile demands. The bonds that assure him he is loved extend be-yond mother and father to relatives, neighbors, teachers, and, above all, his peers. His identifications are derived from these actual rela-tionships and also from fantasy—folk heroes, fictional characters, and public leaders.

From these practical and psychological achievements most children derive sufficient self-esteem to begin the process of detachment from their childhood relationship with their parents. How detachment is conducted depends on the quality of the attachment. Those who feel most dependent on parents may the more fiercely launch themselves away. Those who derive pleasure already from a degree of independence may separate from their parents and construct new kinds of bonds with barely a ripple.

Of middle-class adolescents, for example, only about half go through the emotional storms and nasty rebellions many associate with these years. Of the fifty percent who show evidence of turmoil, again only half have worse than moderate problems with their families, their peers, and, above all, with themselves. On the other hand, lack of any apparent rebelliousness can indicate a failure to face the dilemmas of growing up. Radical departures are made by children who, outwardly at least, show this whole range from no rebellion at all to quite troublesome behavior.

The word "rebellion" summons forth images of unleashed criticism, challenges to parents standards, angry confrontation, and antisocial or dangerous behavior. There is no word that easily substitutes, so I will have to speak of rebellion when I really mean something that can be, and often is, entirely acceptable and even likable. A child who announces his weekend plans instead of asking permission is rebelling. So is a boy who wants his family to switch to nonphosphate detergents, and a girl who says she can do a better job of fixing the lawn mower than her father can. A child is rebelling when he or she discovers Thoreau, true love, or meditation and thinks the older generation knows nothing of such things. Most teen-agers enact much of their rebellion en masse: they dress to irritate, but they all dress the same. Rebellion is a process of distinguishing and distancing oneself from one's parents by probing for difference and disagreement; there need be nothing awful about it.

As teen-agers grow up into young adults their separation is a mutual endeavor. Over time, children's demands for autonomy are matched by parents' willing relinquishment of control. Children come to see themselves more independently, but parents also have to readjust their view of themselves. Mothers and fathers have deeply participated in their child's self for many years. His or her looks, accomplishments, and personality are not just items to take pride in, but partially define who they are too. Women in particular have often lived for and through children. As parents let a son or daughter loosen childhood bonds, they lose something of themselves, and must work to restore it.

Given a long and gradual development toward maturity, parents don't find their task so hard. To be sure, it is difficult at times to have those nice kids who have eaten our cookies and "borrowed" our tools for so many years disagree with our politics ("You're going to vote for *who*?") and, in general, skirt our influence in many everyday matters ("Oh, Mom, you wouldn't understand"). But on the whole most families have the humor to survive a certain amount of criticism in return for the freedom to develop new interests of their own and the gratification of having raised children who can now conduct their own lives. That's as it should be, but it isn't always that way.

No radical departer—not the nine I am using to illustrate the general predicament or any of the hundreds of others I have known—has thus gradually been able to separate from his or her family to everyone's mutual satisfaction. Few have been able to engage their peers in their own form of rebellion, or have sought safety in numbers by rebelling among peers. Some, like Dennis Ericson, enter their 20s without ever having disagreed with their families. They haven't rebelled at all. Others, like Nancy Lewis, don't find ways to control their own lives. They rebel to no effect. And all of them, without exception, are still so closedly tied to their parents either in reality or in fantasy that I will often use the word "children" to refer to joiners in spite of their chronological age. Each has been felled by some obstacle that others their age manage to scramble over, even if it bruises both them and their families for a while.

The process of formulating one's identity is, of course, never over. One is forever having to reformulate oneself to catch up, so to speak, with the changing context as one pursues a career, gets married, becomes a parent, suffers tragedies, grows older. Change is so rapid during adolescence, however, that the task of identity formation then is more demanding than it is likely ever to be again. Also, society demands it of teen-agers whether they like it or not.

Parents withdraw support. They no longer wish to supervise children's homework or to chaperone them everywhere. Even if they wish to, they can no longer control children's aggressive and sexual impulses. So adolescents are forced to a degree of independence. They must arrange their own social lives, care for their own bodies, make many of their own decisions, and begin to earn their own money. They are now too muscularly strong for others to subdue easily; they must take over the control of their physical aggression. Both sexes were able to manage the rather mild sexuality of childhood; now sexual impulses are insistent, unpredictable, and sometimes quite unmanageable.

Parents also make it clear to high-school students that adult responsibilities loom ahead. By 16, students know that their present academic industry will determine which college they can hope to attend. By 18, they are asked to make tentative choices of college curriculum and to articulate their reasons for that choice. Most of them are expected to leave home. By 21, they are required to narrow their career choice either by declaring a major or, if they have gone to junior college, by entering the work force. These challenges are unlike those of childhood: they smack of permanence.

There is some suggestion that families of radical departers are hesitant to withdraw support or relinquish control. Fred Vitelli's father protected his son from the consequences of his delinquencies. Mr. Gould paid Jamie's way even into his mid-20s. Jennifer Green's mother masterminded both her daughter's psyche and her piano career.

At the same time that parents are withdrawing support and control, their sons and daughters are withdrawing the unconditional love for and faith in parents that typifies earlier childhood. But children can't continue into adulthood loveless and faithless. They seek intimacy with others—friends and lovers. Instead of relying on the belief system that was on loan to them during childhood, they now formulate ideologies that will serve the unique person each has come to be.

Of those radical departers toward the upper end of the age group, who might have been expected to enjoy intimacy with a lover, only Kathy O'Connor had a relationship that was more than exploitive or tentative, and her marriage didn't last out the year. Some joiners have no friends at all. They are convinced that peers couldn't possibly understand them—a conviction that certainly precludes intimacy. Those who go through the motions of a social life often use the word "plastic" to describe their relationships. They have no sense of deep connection or even of genuineness with their friends, and can't use their affection and admiration as sources of self-esteem.

No radical departers I have studied felt committed to a value system at the time of their joining. Indeed, to all of them, nothing they were doing made any sense, nor did the activities of others. One could sum up their desolation by saying that radical departers feel they belong with no one, believe in nothing.

This is a risk that is incurred by all adolescents as they sever themselves from childhood. By denigrating the family from whose love and values they have derived the very core of their self-esteem, they may also devalue whatever "good" portion of their self relied on family approval. In other words, they may reject a part of themselves as they reject their parents, and thus find themselves unlovable and of no significance. The trick of withdrawing from the curriculum of a family self is to have built an extracurricular self that is equally laudable.

Most teen-agers do have moments of grave doubt: no one likes them, they're ugly, everything's stupid, what's the sense of even trying? But these are moments only, and give way more and more to positive feelings of accomplishment, significance, and worth. Those who will join radical groups behave as though so great a portion of whatever they have found good about themselves has been built on parental ties that were they to sever them they would be terribly depleted, if not entirely empty. Every joiner I have spoken with was, at the time of his or her departure, at a low of self-esteem so devastating that there seemed to be no self at all.

Teen-agers want—and it is required of them—a self of their very own, unique, authentic, and separate from the selves of parents. By coincidence, the tasks that children must tackle to differentiate, rearrange, and fortify their sense of self all begin with I: Independence, Individuation, Impulse control, Industry, Intimacy, Ideological commitment, and, of course, Identity itself. One might call these the years of the I.

This preoccupation with internal and private psychological issues has led adults to accuse youth of an excess of narcissism. Self-involvement is, however, a trademark of the times. "Develop yourself," Mrs. Green admonished Jennifer, and that theme of self-realization, self-actualization, liberation, and autonomy is echoed throughout the middle class. The message can make individuals ruthlessly oblivious of the needs of others, and blind to the fact of all people's mutual dependency. No wonder youth is selfish, since society demands that it be so.

Worse, by stressing the early achievement of an independent self parents may be out of step with the psychological realities of adolescent development. There seems plenty of evidence from the young people I have worked with, especially those who have made radical departures but also those who have not, that the self is for years tentative and in constant flux. They themselves don't think it can bear much scrutiny.

By demanding that the self be "actualized" prior to reaching the 20s, society is handing children a double-edged sword. With so much attention focused on the self, they tend to protect their fragility with selfishness, egotism, and the kind of acting out Nancy Lewis attempted with her theatrics and precocious "liberation." At the same time, the assumption that they should have no fragility to hide convinces these children that no one else experiences doubt and pain. All nine of these representative radical departers kept their distress secret because they felt "no one would understand."

Again, a modicum of such loneliness is to be expected in adolescence. All through one's life one harbors some core that one knows to be unreachable by others. But adolescents learn that with the effort of reaching out and inviting others to do the same, sufficient intimacy can be found to ease loneliness. Joiners seem to long for a belonging with others that requires no such effort at mutual understanding. Unlike those who, among less judgmental peers at least, become able endlessly to probe, analyze, confess, explore, and lay bare their very souls to one another over these years, radical departers hold aloof while hoping for some unconditional mutual capitulation in which others would not ask a single question. This is their version of belonging.

Joiners' version of belief is equally unconditional. To them an ideology should, without the effort of their own analysis, offer every answer absolutely.

To some extent, longing for the Answer is an inevitable conse-
quence of intellectual maturation. Younger children are poor debaters:
something is either true or false, right or wrong, and if there is an argument it is won by the person with the loudest voice. Adolescents
can step outside themselves to see issues from various vantage points,
and each view, they realize, contains some truth. In Ethan Browning's
school for gifted children, this talent was formalized in a debating club
to which Ethan belonged, and was a point of pride at home, where
right opinions were considered the offspring of free inquiry.

This intellectual experience can be heady, and it can be unsettling. How, if different things have different meanings to different people, can there be any meaning at all? What, down deep, do *I* really
believe? *Who am I? Where am I going?* And *why?*

One can catch Ethan Browning at just that moment of unsettling
awareness. His extensive reading had given him histories of the Cru-
sades and the Inquisition, Oriental philosophies, Kafka, Emerson, and
Death of a Salesman. This array of distraught and dissenting humanity
was discussed around his family's civilized dinner table as though it
were so many specimens to be dissected. Certainly there was something "missing": some heart of the matter that was ultimately undis-
sectible.

This was not the Brownings' particular fault. What is merely intellectual discussion among adult members of the middle class may be
a desperate search for practical and personal applications among their
sons and daughters.

Perhaps too much has been made of the "generation gap"; most
parents are far more able to appreciate their children's concerns than
their children give them credit for. But a rapidly changing world really
does alter perceptions abruptly, particularly for the young, who will
have to track their future among shifting sands. For Kathy O'Connor's
parents, Catholicism had answers for pain and suffering, but as a nurse
Kathy came face to face with the appalling reality of moral dilem-

mas—the "right to die" and the "right to life"—for which there seemed no answers. Jack Ericson had as a soldier defended the Western world from totalitarianism; in what way was that parallel to the ideological issues (if they were that) in Southeast Asia? To the Holtzmans, a liberal arts education was the key to every sort of success, but by 1978, when Phil had completed two years of collegee, liberal arts students faced unemployment after graduation.

The sureties that guided parents no longer seem reliable to children who came of age during recent decades. Half of all marriages now end in divorce. These are the days of dioxin, the population explosion, downward mobility, and the threat of nuclear war. Moreover, these are children of the electronic age.

It must often look to them as if adults' daily concerns—which brand of toaster to choose, whether to buy more life insurance, how to get into the best college—are sheer insanity. How can parents, who once seemed so strong and wise, not be *doing* something to make the world safe for their children?

They are, of course, doing the best they know how. They understand the many reasons why they can't cut through the Gordian knot of ethical and practical dilemmas with one neat slice of an answer. To a 16-year-old, however, parents begin to look like fallen idols. This is especially so among the families from whom radical departers come, and it is owing to the mixed messages they give.

While organizing rescue for starving Africans, Jamie Gould's mother enjoyed her porcelains and Persian cats. While espousing honesty, churchgoing Mr. Browning was observed by Ethan to be fudging his income tax. Mrs. Green flirted with radical dreams while pushing the orthodox virtues of daily four-hour piano practice for Jennifer. Middle-class children are often raised with a gloss of idealism that their parents hope they will have the sense not to take too literally as they reach adulthood.

Most do have that good sense. As they separate, adolescents put their parents through their paces: they challenge, provoke, argue, and criticize. They adopt moral stances of their own, which are both extreme, to make a point, and tentative, to test the waters. But the common result is that they gradually define the boundaries of their own and their parents' capabilities and limitations, keep whatever portions of the family's value system seem workable to them, add snippets of personal ideals that seem to be proved out through their own experimentation, and come through the trial without any prolonged crisis of belief. They become willing, in other words, to face the personal and public moral dilemmas that no ideology can guarantee against.

In contrast, joiners look to belief as a way to avoid any personal dilemma at all. Feeling so little self-esteem, they can't shoulder the responsibility of perhaps making a wrong moral choice and thereby feeling more worthless still. They hope for an ideology that will bolster the "good me," that part of them which is admirable to themselves. They long to be purged of all badness, to be pure—and this their parents cannot do for them.

Parents have, in fact, few outward clues that might warn them of an impending departure. Joiners closely guard the secret of their inner desolation. Even as their unhappiness mounts to critical proportions they may continue to, as so many put it, "go through the motions" of whatever has been their accustomed life. Only in the few months—sometimes mere weeks—before their departure do families notice a visible decline in buoyancy that marks their inner sinking. Before then, they have seemed to be in a steady state. And that's what should be the giveaway.

While other children, tumultuously or uneventfully, are piecing together their separate selves, those who will join radical groups are peculiarly stalled. Whatever they are like, they have been that way for years. Others are learning to say "I know who I am"; these children gain no notion of what a self might feel like. Most young adults begin to need others and to feel needed, love others and feel loved; potential joiners remain bereft. While their peers are becoming increasingly captivated by all sorts of interests, they become weighted with tedium or aimlessly adrift. By the time the overwhelming proportion of adolescents enters the 20s, these young men and women have a sense of optimism and enthusiasm for their future. Radical departers have been unable to conceive of a future for themselves.

And then the future presents itself. Out of the blue, the Hare Krishna, Divine Light Mission, Healing Workshop, Children of God, or Armed Guard offers on a silver platter every ingredient that has been missing from their unhappy youth.

3

Breaking Away

What distinguishes a radical departer from other adolescents and young adults can be minimized by saying that it is all a matter of degree. This is to some extent true, since all people must experience self-doubt, disillusion, loneliness, and uncertainty, especially on the way to adulthood. Usually, however, such feelings are felt in sequence. A 15-year-old may worry about her looks, but by the time she discovers the degree of corruption in the world she at least thinks she's attractive. A freshman in college may feel isolated during the first weeks, but by the time he discovers he has no idea what to major in, he is part of a friendship group that vocally shares his uncertainty. Radical departers are notable not only for the degree of their pain, but also for the fact that everything seems to hit them at once. Too much has been put off; the debris of stagnation has accumulated. They open the dam of their own development by the abrupt and violent breaking away that is a radical departure.

The confluence of unfaced dilemmas in this developmental logjam can be considered a critical period. Some other children suffer such a critical period too, but don't join the Moonies. The final ingredient that makes for a radical departure is an accident. At just this critical period in their lives, all of these unhappy children are offered what seems to them a magical solution: separation without concomitant pain. As in a fairy tale, each is handed what he or she takes to be the key to heaven. Although each story is superficially different—and I will use each to emphasize a different aspect of joiners' experience upon breaking away—the themes that color one tale color all radical departures.

Philip Holtzman was everything his parents expected him to be, yet "for all my successes," he explained, "I never felt that I had control, *real* control, over what I was doing or what was happening to me. I was succeeding, I was doing well. I found it easy to achieve in school, and in sports, and with girls. But it's not as if any of this turned me on. Nothing did. I was just going through the motions."

Locked into the expectations of his parents, teachers, and friends, Phil felt his actions were in the nature of a command performance put on for the benefit of others. His easy success had become a kind of tyranny, expected *of* him but not emanating *from* him. His only stab at drawing the line somewhere between himself and his parents was his avowed disconnection from Judaism, but this modest attempt at rebellion was no more than stamping a foot and saying no. Refusing to accompany his mother and father to temple did not stop the waves of expectation he passively rode.

He began to doubt whether he could take charge of his life even if given the opportunity. Many of those who join radical groups express this sense of powerlessness. Phil said he had felt like a pawn in an incomprehensible chess game that was being played by others more powerful and more devious than he. In this game, it seemed to him, he was moved from square to square in a strategy he didn't understand, and no matter where he found himself, he had, as he put it, a sense of "not being there." One can appreciate the irony of his predicament: in order to take control of his own life, he had to fail his parents.

Phil left home that July for his "educational" year abroad. Perhaps he intended the trip as a gesture toward independence, but his parents saw it as the next step in the game plan and paid his way. He was to get a job in Europe by fall to help out. He stayed in hostels and inexpensive hotels that catered to his peers. He met students from Germany, Scandinavia, Britain, France, Brazil, and India. Drugs and sex were freely available to him; the sheer abundance and diversity excited but unnerved him. By August the gloss of hedonism had already given way to increasing feelings of futility.

Finally, in September, Phil hoped to get a grip on himself by starting work. An exceptional skier, he got a job as instructor in Kitzbühel, to begin at the end of November. With over two months of time still on his hands, he decided—"what the hell," was all he could offer as an explanation—to go to Israel. His parents had talked about that promised land often enough. Considering that he had disappointed his parents in only one way—his lack of commitment to Judaism—his choice of Israel might have struck him as remarkable, but without wondering any further about it, he rationalized that the weather was beautiful there in the autumn, and the girls were rumored to be earthy and uncomplicated.

On a clear, warm Friday evening in Jerusalem, Phil decided to watch the religious Jews praying at the ancient western wall in the Old City, called the "Wailing Wall." The wall, a remnant of the Second Temple, destroyed by the Romans, is considered a holy site by religious Jews everywhere. Phil had been walking around the city all day. His red hair lay damp over his forehead; his feet ached. He remembered thinking that afternoon that he had to find some direction for his life, that he couldn't continue as he had been, feeling "crappy" about himself.

The Wailing Wall is hauntingly beautiful in the evening. Phil was fascinated by the spectacle of hundreds of religious Jews of all ages engrossed in prayer, and tourists hushed by their reverence. He used the word "spiritual" to describe his mood, and both the feeling and the word on his lips surprised him. As he stood there in the failing but uniquely golden light of Jerusalem, physically tired, unsettled, inexplicably moved, a young man dressed in jeans and wearing a skullcap approached him. The conversation was laconic.

"Hi."

"Hello."

"You like this?"

"It's beautiful."

"We have it all the time at the yeshiva."

This was Phil's first encounter with Zev, a transplanted Canadian and now a member of a yeshiva, an Orthodox Jewish seminary. He invited Phil to come over to their house, where "a whole bunch of us" would be celebrating *Oneg Shabbat*, the ritual held each Friday at sundown to greet the arrival of the Sabbath.

Echoing his "what the hell" reason for visiting Israel in the first place, Phil recalled a "What do I have to lose?" response to Zev's invitation.

The evening turned out to be an overwhelming experience. Phil had never before seen such genuine joy—another word that came surprisingly to his lips. Boys and girls in their early 20s prayed, ate, and sang together with abandon, happiness, and a dedication that moved him utterly. This scene was passionate, but not sexual; the boys and girls were not allowed to touch one another. Phil was infused with love and the celebration of life.

The members of the yeshiva were all English-speaking. They, like Phil, had come to Israel as tourists with nothing more serious in mind than sightseeing. None of them was from a religious background; all had been raised in warm families and comfortable homes. They called their joining of the yeshiva "God's will," as though they had not even had to exercise a choice, A sense of great relief enveloped Phil.

One week later, Philip Holtzman phoned his parents to tell them he wasn't taking the job as a ski instructor in Switzerland, he wasn't going back to school, and he wasn't coming home—maybe ever.

Making a radical departure while away from home, sometimes for the first time, is common. The actual physical separation from the family seemed to prove more unnerving to Phil and others than they had anticipated. I think Phil may even have felt his parents' compliance with his plans to be an abandonment. There is a terrible conflict. These children wish to be back home, safe from the frightening freedoms of travel, but then how can they be separate? Separate, they feel empty—a word used frequently by radical departers—as though there is not enough self to fill them. Phil's is the clearest case of a compromise solution to this conflict.

By choosing a flight into the yeshiva, he "came home" to Judaism an ocean apart from his family. In his eyes, he was not failing them either, since he was conforming to their deep wish that he be faithful to Jewish tradition. But—and this amazed him—his parents received his telephone call with all the pain and anger parents feel when their child rebels with animosity. Phil, innocent of knowing that out-orthodoxing his parents was tantamount to scathing criticism, had found a painless way to initiate the rebellion he had deferred for many years.

Dennis Ericson's breaking away from his family was quite similar. Like Phil, Dennis had an urge to "get away" into what he at first thought of as the "adventure and excitement" of joining the army during the Vietnam War. He was having a hard time living out his family's mythology about him. Although he was their conservative standard-bearer in a liberal university climate, Dennis felt he was living a lie. The outspoken political opinions with which he buttressed arguments with his fellow students were not heartfelt. They were, after all, his father's. The excitement a person feels when he has forged his opinions through the work of his own experience and intellect was lacking. "I argued with the peaceniks," Dennis informed me, "but I envied their spirit."

The same sense of being family-manufactured instead of self-made robbed Dennis of pleasure in his studies. He felt he was on a conveyor belt taking him along the same route to engineering his father and older brother had traveled before him. Drifting with this spuriously assembled self, he was unhappy but felt he "shouldn't" be. When parents are happy with their child, how is the child to feel justified in being unhappy with himself? It is typical of radical departers that they nurture and protect a negative uniqueness: no one is so empty as they are, no one would understand.

The Ericsons themselves provided the opening in this wall of presumptions about the sort of person Dennis was by their inconsistent response to his wish to be drafted. Their prowar stance was at odds with their not wanting their own son to go to war, and into this crack he drove the wedge of his determination to be drafted.

When Dennis did get his "greetings" from Uncle Sam, the essential fragility of his gung-ho attitude became evident. He no longer echoed the militaristic sentiments he had espoused in unison with his father.

He got in touch with the New Left, a campus club that had become part of an underground railroad smuggling young men from the United States into Canada on false papers. He was routed to Vancouver, where, along with a growing community of draft dodgers and deserters, he lived in an urban commune made up of just those angry peaceniks he had argued with only weeks before. The whole switch from war apologist to exiled draft dodger took six weeks, and left Dennis and his parents equally bewildered. Neither he nor they could understand this change of heart, as though both had developed a sudden amnesia about its source: the Ericsons' inconsistent wish for their son's safety.

Dennis went looking to buy a *futon*, the Japanese mattress favored as an inexpensive bed by his commune. The health-food store where *futons* were sold was run by two men and three women, all young and attractive. They wore white turbans and clothing, and spoke politely and gently. He was at first put off by their alien appearance—he himself was the sturdy, crew-cut epitome of conservatism—but found them strangely "relaxing" and "encouraging." There was an air of peace around these odd shopkeepers.

His own attraction to them surprised Dennis. If he'd met these devotees of an exotic religious philosophy only two months earlier, when Nixon, Vietnam, engineering, and the Young Republicans had seemed the natural order of the world, he would have thought they were crazy.

He kept going back to that store on slight excuses over the next three weeks. Each time, he had the feeling that he didn't want to leave this group of people, and that they didn't want him to leave them.

A month later, he joined these five and about 200 other disciples in the Healthy Happy Holy Organization—3H0.

The bafflement Dennis felt by his own actions points to a problem these youngsters have. Whereas they are aware that they are not the person their parents wish them to be, they have not yet arrived at any alternative. Parents are shocked that their son or daughter has done something entirely "out of character," because they have known only the manufactured version of their child. It's not their fault; Dennis and Phil never had any other face to show. Yet radical departers, before they join their groups, think of themselves as frauds. This was especially true of the two most talented girls among the nine examples: Jennifer Green, who was so brilliant a pianist, and Suzanne Marquette, on her way to becoming a professional skater.

Just as Dennis's and Phil's selves had been ordained by family expectations rather than forged by the individual, Jennifer was her mother's product. Mrs. Green participated in her musical career as though it were her own. The more disinterested and disinclined to practice Jennifer became over the months before her departure, the more her mother praised her talent and assumed her future as a concert pianist. She spoke often of Jennifer's beauty and intelligence. But at the same time she was giving a quite different message. Those four years of constant dwelling on the need for psychotherapy convinced Jennifer that she must be weaker than others, defective in some way. The more her mother remarked on her looks, intellect, and talent against the worrisome background of "needing help," the more Jennifer doubted her mother's motives and the veracity of her pronouncements. She was so overwhelmed by this barrage of interpretation, this definition by another of who she was, what she was like, what was good about her and what was wrong with her, that she couldn't find anything genuine of her own. Unless she were to see her mother as flawed—a finding this dependent child couldn't welcome—she could only assume that she had taken her mother in; she was a fraud.

Intimacy with her mother prevented the distance Jennifer needed in order to sort things out for herself, and in the Green family—and many other joiners' families also, I believe—a rather tuned-out father contributed to her dilemma. Fathers at this point in a child's development often step between mother and child in a helpful way. They are frequently the one to encourage new skills—driving a car or getting a job—that emphasize independence. They extend invitations to become interested in the outside world of politics, economics, science, sports, or history. Mr. Green did not. He saw his wife and daughter as united in efforts that were either inconsequential to him, such as "self-realization," or beyond his scope, such as Jennifer's career in music. Just when Jennifer could have used some distance from her mother, he threw up his hands—and threw them together.

At the time Jennifer made her radical departure, the crisis of committing herself to one of two internationally famous conservatories that were vying for her was looming. To Mrs. Green, this was the culmination of years of her devotion to her daughter's talent; to Jennifer, it was the final encasing in a mold she had to break out of.

Leafing through one of the many magazines on popular psychology to which her mother subscribed, Jennifer came upon the following ad:

> Confused? Aimless? Drifting?
> Join our therapeutic commune.
> Come and live at the Healing Workshop.

Jennifer answered the ad immediately, and received by return mail a brochure outlining the program, along with a handwritten invitation to visit the group outside Taos, New Mexico. She told her mother about it. Mrs. Green had mixed feelings. On the one hand, she would have liked to spend time with such a group herself had she not been needed at home; on the other hand, she wanted to check out this intriguing new therapy before encouraging Jennifer to accept the invitation. Jennifer, she insisted, must certainly continue her preparation for the conservatory.

As it turned out, there was nothing Mrs. Green could check out— the group was little known—and Jennifer, gray eyes steady in her perfect face, was adamant. Jennifer visited the Healing Workshop the following week, feeling nervous but somewhat defended by skepticism. Remarkably, both feelings were allayed within minutes. As soon as she entered the adobe office in this exhilaratingly beautiful spot—the breathtaking setting of desert backed by mountain—she was greeted by Kurt, the director.

She told me that Kurt was the most beautiful man she had ever seen—tall, muscular, bronzed, with a craggy face and ginger beard. When he kissed her hand and extended his personal welcome, she came near to "swooning," to use her word. When she related this, her cheeks flushed, and she said that she couldn't describe that initial feeling any better. To her, the program was rich icing on a perfect cake—one long encounter group in which every member of the commune was intensely involved and to which all were ecstatically committed.

She phoned her parents to tell them that she'd found what she had been searching for, and what was missing in her life—not that she had ever confided that so much was missing. She added that she would not be returning home and didn't expect to continue her education in the foreseeable future. She was giving up the piano.

The timing of a radical departure is not haphazard. Against the backdrop of these joiners' escalating sense of fraudulence, there is an event that threatens to expose them: Philip Holtzman's failure really to make anything of his "educational" months in Europe, the prospect that Dennis Ericson would have to back up his militaristic stance on the battlefields of Vietnam, Jennifer Green's impending enrollment in a conservatory.

Suzanne Marquette's radical departure occurred just after she had successfully auditioned for the ice show.

"Except for being a good skater," Suzanne was to recall of that time, "I had no idea of what I wanted in my life, nor of what I could do. I remember arguing with my friends about the future of all things; none of us had any idea of where we were going, or what our world was going to be like in a few years. My mother would do anything for me then, but she couldn't begin to understand my unhappiness. I felt that every time I broached the subject I was stabbing her in the back. Keep smiling, I told myself."

Suzanne programed her days from dawn to dark. She buried herself in a crescendo of skating practice, volunteer work, household chores, and care of her twin brothers—anything to avoid the painful emptiness that free time engendered. It would have been difficult for Mrs. Marquette to see any warning signal in this; she too used busyness as an analgesic.

For all her self-imposed organization, Suzanne began to feel trapped. She loved skating, but the grueling hours of practice had evolved into a taxing ritual, one that she paradoxically hung onto for dear life. She told me that she had suffered at this time an uneasy feeling that if she gave up any of her activities, everything around her would come crashing down. She felt that her life was a brittle superstructure that had no foundation to support her or the weight of her future.

Suzanne's story is particularly poignant because her perceptions were so much at odds with how others saw her. Reaching toward the spotlight of the professional skater, pretty as a picture, with her blond hair, innocent eyes, and small, lithe figure, she might easily have been envied by other girls were it not that she disarmed them with her natural charm. To her family and to her friends, she seemed poised on the brink of success at the very moment that she felt most threatened by it. So this capable girl, unflaggingly responsible and focused on her work, was sent alone to Santa Monica from her home in Minneapolis for the skating audition. She was to audition on a Thursday, remain at a hotel in Santa Monica over the weekend and return to Minneapolis Monday, just after the results of the auditions were to be announced.

Suzanne lay on the beach near her hotel that summer morning working on her tan and killing time before her 2:00 P.M. audition. She was feeling drowsy. She heard voices talking and singing softly, but it was as if she were dreaming. When she looked up she saw John, Rich, and Anna. She recalled for me how beautiful they looked in the sun, how happy. Their eyes met, and Anna invited her over. Still drowsy and dreamlike, Suzanne just gazed at them; the three got up and approached her.

They spread their blanket, poured juice for her, and again started singing softly to a guitar. And smiling, always smiling, warm, friendly, safe. Suzanne had been warned by her parents to be wary of strangers in California—it was a far cry from Minneapolis—but there was no hint of threat, no drugs or sex. "Just peace," Suzanne explained.

She remembered that they sang and talked and laughed together for several hours. Anna invited her to rejoin them in the evening, when she could meet their friends and share good food with them. Suzanne felt soothed but unsure—until after her audition.

The audition went extremely well. Although she chose not to dwell on its significance, her success meant that she was about to graduate from childhood into the adult world of the paid professional, on tour, away from home, responsible for herself. She took her new friends up on their invitation.

They hadn't done justice to the beach house they had described to her. It was a gorgeous wooden mansion, a gem in the dramatic setting of the Pacific coast. Suzanne was greeted by Anna and John and a host of young people, who were so happy that she was soon as relaxed as she had been on the beach. A long table was laden with all kinds of fresh fruits and salads; the music wafting through the house was about love and hope and caring for one another. It was a magical evening.

As she reluctantly made ready to return to her hotel room, the group said she could come back the next morning to go with them to their country retreat in northern California for a long weekend. She did.

Suzanne phoned her parents to tell them the results of her trip the Monday after that weekend. She had passed the audition. But she was not going to join the ice show; she wouldn't be on the flight home. She had joined the Unification Church. She was a Moonie. She had never felt like this before, she told her mother—uplifted, excited. The Marquettes were appalled.

If the makings of melodrama were not so blatant, if potential tragedy were not lurking in the background, I would have been amused by the vast differences in perception of the same events experienced by parents and their children. Every one of these young men and women who were having such a hard time feeling good about themselves at the time they broke away was certain that his or her parents were oblivious to his or her sufferings.

Philip Holtzman at the time he was feeling alienated, demoralized, useless, and empty "knew" his mother and father perceived him as a born leader, happy, creative, self-reliant, confident, and optimistic. Dennis was sure the whole Ericson family was taken in by his fraudulent front. Jennifer Green and Suzanne Marquette were convinced their unhappiness was so unique, and so secret, that their parents had noticed nothing. On the other hand, radical departers expect their families to be as delighted by their choice as they are.

The fact is that all the sets of parents I spoke with had noticed that something was amiss. Dennis had appeared unnaturally agitated to the Ericsons; Phil had seemed uneasy and dispirited. Mrs. Green had noticed for months that Jennifer had no enthusiasm for the piano; her daughter had even voiced her thought that she might "give the whole thing up." Suzanne said the same about skating to Mrs. Marquette, and for a girl who had always been so spirited, her busyness had recently seemed to be robotlike.

The odd thing is that the difference in perception is not in how, say, Phil and the Holtzmans perceived him—both he and his parents were aware of his unhappiness. The discrepancy is in Phil's and all these children's total misreading of their parents.

I have wondered what it is about this misreading that might be self-protective. If a child's unhappiness seems to him the *only* unique or genuine aspect of his personality, he may cling to that scrap of self as though to reveal it were to be wiped out altogether. Or perhaps what he is clinging to is the front itself, and were he to admit the emptiness in back of it the scaffolding would, as Suzanne put it, "come crashing down." One can look at it either way. The fact is that none of these boys and girls confided to family or friends.

And the trouble is that, even though there are signs of deep distress, there is no clue to the direction the child will take to relieve it. Not only those who break away from their families in a radical departure go through a critical period in which all the possible strands that lead to adulthood seem to become impossibly knotted all at once. Some in their critical period will work through the tangle by joining other idealistic movements—the Peace Corps is one—by going through therapy, by finally getting "turned on" to school, to a new interest, or to a lover, or just by sticking it out. That one such person finds an acceptable solution while another takes a radical detour is an accident.

Just at the height of the critical time, when a child is most vulnerable—and especially when he is frightened by an event that has the meaning of impending adulthood—the opportunity to join a radical group is offered. It is unlikely that Ethan Browning, for example, would have joined the Hare Krishna were the temple not just down the street from his home.

The change that the Brownings noticed in Ethan's behavior preceded by only weeks his breaking away. This intense and intellectually gifted 16-year-old had staved off loneliness for years by attacking his interests with vigor. This was not unlike how Mr. Browning approached life, with a singularly intense drive to learn, compete, and succeed. But whereas his father derived satisfaction from his devotion to business and the Episcopalian church, for some weeks the family had been aware that Ethan had given up chess and sailing, and that he had lost his zest for study. Ethan described the sort of person he felt himself to be just prior to those final weeks.

"I couldn't relate to any of the kids in school. I had one friend, but maybe even he thought I was a little peculiar. I sure wasn't part of any gang. It wasn't that I was sad, or even that I felt lonely. I had my interests, and I enjoyed them. In sailing and chess though, my opponents were more like foils than comrades. I never got to know any of them, and actually they didn't seem to like me. What I did notice was that my feelings and thoughts seemed different from anybody else's. It was as if they were so unique that nobody my age shared them. Certainly nobody wanted to talk about the philosophical issues I was most concerned about. My parents did, but they were entrenched in their own religion."

In the final weeks, his discomfort became acute. He described emptiness that couldn't be filled. He felt insignificant, irrelevant. And it was not just himself: nobody, not even his "big shot" father, as Ethan called him, seemed to count. The move from suburb to town house in Boston—the move his family thought wouldn't bother him because he was so little engaged in suburban life anyway—left him feeling more isolated than ever. In the midst of a busy world, Ethan thought that he alone was disinvolved.

One day, while walking home past the Hare Krishna temple on his usual route from school, a chanting group of yellow-robed dancers came to a stop in front of him.

"You're Ethan, aren't you?" one asked, smiling. They had seen him before; he had tried to look inside the temple, surreptitiously, he thought. They had learned his name from other students. The group kindly invited him into their temple.

Ethan found the people and their temple fascinating. The beautiful stone building had once been an Episcopalian church (an echo of another ironic homecoming). The members were not at all as strange as they seemed during their street rituals. They struck him as peaceful and relaxed; he described them to me as "down-to-earth and friendly." He watched some of them clean the temple while others talked, prayed, chanted, or prepared food. He was invited to return for dinner the following night.

He accepted on the provision that his parents give their permission. That they did is not surprising. Almost all these families encourage a broad range of interests in their children, expect them to be sharply inquiring of the world, and hope that intellectual freedom will result in independent minds. Mr. Browning therefore took Ethan's attraction to the Hare Krishna to be an extension of the philosophical studies he had so long pursued.

Although the father realized his mistake almost at once, it was too late. Ethan joined the Hare Krishna and moved into the temple down the street after three arduous weeks of strife at home.

Adults tend to look with a certain good-humored condescension on adolescent attempts to believe in something absolute. Most, even those who are as devoted to their church as Ethan's parents were, are aware that any system of belief provides only partial guidance in life's dilemmas. Religion seldom speaks to the sorts of choices that must be made in the business world; anarchism has nothing to say about marital difficulties. Adults manage to keep their belief systems somewhat separate from everyday affairs, to draw upon them only as they seem pertinent, and to mix them liberally with doses of pragmatism. To effect this psychological separation of church and state, so to speak, requires a high degree of self-esteem. The individual must be assured that lapses in charity, for example, don't make him a bad person.

Adolescents in general, and those who make radical departures in particular, have pretty shaky self-esteem. The lower their self-esteem, the more they look to the adult world to tell them how to be good. Inevitably, in middle-class families in which children like Ethan have been raised, no such answer is forthcoming. Their disillusion is acute. Ethan saw his father as a hypocrite. How often have we heard that from our teen-agers! There seemed to be no leader making the world "safe for humanity," no one to trust, no sense to anything.

Perhaps adults don't make enough of their devotion to their beliefs; the absolutism of fundamentalist religions does seem to protect children from radical departures. But it is also true that these children ask too much of belief. They want everything to make sense and to be just; they want themselves and their parents to be perfectly good. Yet part of growing up is coming to terms with the imperfections of people one loves and of the world itself. This, radical departers have been unable to do; all are desperate for Belief.

This is true even of those who seem to be the most sophisticated and cynical: Jamie Gould, too rich to work at anything; Fred Vitelli, rude, selfish, cocksure, and contemptuous of everyone; and Nancy Lewis, with her melodramatic "grande artiste" pretensions.

"Nothing turned me on," Jamie said of the days before he joined the Church of Scientology. "And while I blamed myself for feeling this way, I couldn't make much sense of my friends' lives either. It all seemed so pointless to me: work your ass off in school in order to join a pressured rat race. That to me was the epitome of nonsense. I believed in nothing. I felt like I was living in a phony world. I knew that I was loaded, so I couldn't see the point of getting into that vicious cycle of working and earning. I didn't want to end up like my father, rich, powerful, and unhappy—as far as I could tell. Having all that money actually embarrassed me; I never spoke about it to people who didn't know my background."

The rich, like the beautiful, can be peculiarly handicapped in their search for personal significance. Most 26-year-olds can measure themselves by real earnings; everything was given to Jamie. At the same time, he had no goals other than to avoid being like his father, and if this was a try at formulating a separate self, it wasn't much of a one, since Jamie accepted from Mr. Gould the handsome monthly allowance and income from the trust fund that paid for his luxurious life style in his New York City house. He couldn't even afford to criticize his father to his face; he was too dependent on his largesse. He knew himself to be a hypocrite, and despised himself.

In the midst of Jamie's turmoil a friend suggested psychotherapy. Many of these young people are not ready for "help." Jamie, for instance, saw psychotherapists as agents of his absentee family who were paid to mold children to parental expectations. Also, like Jennifer Green, they don't want to confirm their suspicions that something is "wrong" with them. They are frightened. They sense the thinness of their façade and the flimsiness of their defenses, and are aware that probing painful areas could be more than they could take. Jamie was "against" psychotherapy in a blanket fashion.

Therefore, when he came upon a group of young people demonstrating in the streets against psychiatry, he was stirred to listen to their words.

What they said seemed to make sense; they were even more critical than he was, but more moving than the words they spoke was the enthusiasm and involvement they showed.

He lingered longer than anyone else in the rapidly changing audience, and he was noticed. An appealing girl approached him, and asked him if he knew anything about Scientology. Another cult, Jamie recalled thinking, but he was willing to hear her out. As she continued, he was first drawn to her dedication and warmth, then stimulated by her concept of the mind. She wasn't a zealot, he recalled reassuring himself, she was friendly, wishing to discuss, not wanting to proselytize.

Another young man joined them and asked if Jamie would like to visit their center after the demonstration was over. He accepted, and walked back with them the few blocks to their offices. Once there, he was thoroughly impressed by what he saw. These young men and women were so unlike him. They were focused, purposeful, and strong. They explained to him the heady theories of their leader, L. Ron Hubbard; these ideas left Jamie "high."

Jamie Gould joined the Church of Scientology later that same week.

The accidental way in which a person can stumble out of cynicism and into belief is most vividly shown by Fred Vitelli's experience. Fred, alone among the nine followed here, was not aware that he was missing anything until he was at the very brink of his departure.

"I think of those days with embarrassment. What an asshole I was. I guess that everybody thought that I was obnoxious, and I used to look down on everyone else. I thought they were suckers. And it wasn't an act—I genuinely felt that way. I went along my merry way without thinking.

"It wasn't as if I was sold on a more worthwhile course; it was just that I *knew* no harm could possibly befall me. I'd learned that no matter what trouble I could get into, my father would always bail me out, and I'd end up in better shape than ever. I didn't have to do anything constructive, and so I didn't."

Fred did, however, entertain grandiose fantasies about pulling off some coup in the business world to rival his parents' success, although, far from pulling a coup, they had worked hard gradually to build their family business into the large corporation it now was. Perhaps his own fantasy set him up for his departure, because he found that being stoned in Europe brought him no closer to "making a killing"—at least not in commerce. No plan occurred to him, and Fred only then began to feel uneasy.

He admitted that it was his habitual preoccupation with "getting laid" that first made him notice a ravishing girl deeply involved in conversation with a group of young men and women in an outdoor café in Rome (where else for a good Italian boy?) on a beautiful, sunny autumn day. This was a bright, well-heeled group, he thought, as he continued to look over his "prey," who seemed to be leading the animated discussion. Though intense and obviously serious, the youthful participants seemed to be enjoying themselves. They spoke in English, French, Italian, and German amid emotional exclamations lubricated by generous amounts of wine.

The girl's eyes met his. Fred strolled by their table to ask some inane question.

Yvette beckoned him in impeccable but heavily French-accented English to sit down, and they began talking spontaneously and easily. But she never lost track of the political discussion, which had to do with NATO's deployment of American nuclear weapons on European soil and possible mass public demonstrations which this group, the Armed Guard, might help instigate or organize.

Fred, who heretofore had been bored by more than ten minutes of serious discussion, was riveted as much by the conversation as by Yvette.

These people had plans, big ones, important ones. He felt engrossed and enthusiastic for the first time in his life, he told me.

He spent that night with Yvette, and stayed with her when, several days later, this militant leftist group of anarchists traveled from Rome to their farm retreat in northern Italy.

Through his affair with Yvette, he became a member of the secretive and suspicious Armed Guard, and phoned his parents to tell them of his radical departure.

One of the signs of distress in an adolescent's life is this sudden and compelling urge, felt by Fred as well as by Phil and Dennis, to "get away from it all." The urge is not the same as that expressed by college students who wish to study in their field at a particular institute abroad, or to go skiing for a week in the winter holiday with friends, or to take a leave of absence from college for work experience. There is a certain vagueness in their plans—no particular destination or itinerary, no explanation of exactly what it is they wish to do once they are there. The urgency is in the leave-taking itself. Nancy Lewis exemplifies both that gnawing drive simply to "split" and its aimless character, which, in minutes, becomes focused in an accidental encounter with a radical group.

Nancy had nagged her mother for weeks. She had to, she insisted, "leave all this behind me." "All this" referred of course to strife at home over drugs, her overnight disappearances, her sometime boyfriend, and the unsavory actor from whom she took drama lessons. But "all this" also included Nancy's state of mind.

"I didn't know what my parents wanted from me. Their expectations made no sense to me. The rules that they said I had to live by just didn't seem to apply to me. They didn't understand me, and I didn't understand them. I remember thinking that there was no point in breaking my ass at business school or anything else, because it wouldn't do any good. I wouldn't fit into the 'right' mold anyway."

For all her aspirations for the life of an artist, Nancy had strong doubts that she had any real talent. It was largely a façade; bravado in the service of self-protection. She felt isolated from the mainstream of her peers who had continued in college, and from her workaday parents.

She felt that playing the game the way she was supposed to might expose her to failure and ridicule, even humiliation. She cultivated a sense of futility, of fatalism. She couldn't rely on adults' values, which often made no sense to her; if she tried to, they wouldn't work for *her* anyway. She was quite convinced that nothing she could do would make any difference to herself, or to anyone else.

A vacation that winter couldn't come soon enough for Nancy. Sour and truculent but running out of ways to blame her family for her stagnating "career" as an actress, she felt that a big load had been lifted from her shoulders as soon as she and her friend Flo were airborne on the way to Fort Lauderdale. They smoked grass in the rest room during their flight in anticipation of the carefree weeks they were to enjoy. Doing what? They didn't know.

In Fort Lauderdale, it rained for days and there was nothing to do. On the fifth day while Flo was upstairs in their room and Nancy was hanging out in the hotel lobby dressed in her usual provocatively theatrical style, she noticed a bunch of kids sitting on the floor and sofas, laughing and talking. They didn't avert their gaze when she looked at them; rather, they smiled and waved, beckoning her over.

Nancy asked one of the group if he had a joint.

They didn't smoke grass, a young man named Jack replied.

Nancy thought that he was "putting her on," and she responded with a clever retort.

It was strangely quiet; the others smiled, but nobody laughed at her failed attempt at humor. Jack began to chat with her easily, and in a surprisingly friendly manner. She was in drama. He used to be in drama too; the group of friends were working on a play. She could join them in their rehearsal that night.

As Nancy recalled the simplicity of their invitation and their lack of reproach, she remembered thinking that these clean-cut kids were kind of square, and yet she felt gripped and excited by their simplicity and "purity." They were so clean, so sincere, and their friendliness was as open as their smiles.

Flo thought that Nancy was crazy; she had met a couple of guys they could go out with and have a ball.

But Nancy went to the rehearsal.

It wasn't quite a rehearsal, as it turned out. Instead, it was a gathering of a large group of young people to discuss the production of a Passion play. The meeting was held in a ramshackle social hall not far from the Fort Lauderdale airport. The noise, the traffic, the smells, the physical setting were anything but conducive to a spiritual experience, but it didn't seem to matter. Nancy had never seen such intensity and dedication. These were the kind of goody-goodies she usually abhorred, yet there was something so exciting about this scene. After the discussion, which lasted about an hour, they all got down on their knees and prayed together to Jesus and to their spiritual leader, the Reverend David "Moses" Berg, whom they lovingly called "Uncle Mo." Jack, so mild that afternoon, was clearly the leader, urging and exhorting them to serve the Lord. Nancy was deeply impressed.

Prayers were followed by singing and a communal supper. Many of the people there came over and welcomed her, expressing pleasure that she was there. Nancy found herself flooded with warmth and happiness.

Forty-eight hours later Nancy announced her decision to join the Children of God.

Young adults like Fred, Jamie, and Nancy had already begun their rebellions, but they were feeble ones. Jamie wore his earring as a provocative badge of difference from his father, but other than that he had stagnated for years. His "independence" was an accident of wealth. Fred's general nastiness may have struck people as rebellious, but since his father always bailed him out of trouble, he was really as dependent as a child, and felt he could barely make a dent no matter what he did. Nancy played at dissension with her family unconvinced that she had what it takes either to be a real actress in the outside world or to be anything but an actress within her family. These three, more than any of the others, were ultimately able to articulate to me those passages of cynicism, self-hatred, and lack of anchor in relationships that I have quoted. They were separated only in the sense that they had cast themselves adrift from loving relationships.

It was rare to find among the radical departures I studied any joiners who were involved in mature love relationships at the time of their breaking away. On the other hand, they had, compared with their contemporaries, unusually close relationships with their parents—not always loving ones, to be sure, but dependent and undifferentiated, like the relationships of much younger children. The process of breaking away gradually was just not being accomplished—had barely been begun—and a violent wrenching away had to occur in order to get on with growing up. But in these last few stories it can be seen that what little separation joiners, like Jamie, had been capable of had left them painfully lonely, unloving, outside any sense of belonging to anything at all. How can they go further still when the pain is already nearly unbearable?

Kathy O'Connor makes their solution clear. She broke away from her family by finding union with others. So do all radical departers.

Kathy came from the only really devout family in this sample. The O'Connors had what she described as "blind faith in the religious righteousness and morality of all their ideas and actions. As far as they were concerned, there was no other way. They really believed 'the meek shall inherit the earth.' I also couldn't understand how they could have such overriding trust in our politicians." She admitted, however, that she had kept her mother and father on a pedestal throughout childhood and adolescence. She had learned her ideals of selfless charity at their knee and never doubted their wisdom and benevolence even when she was of college age.

This isn't usual even for a 6-year-old these days. Few middle-class boys and girls are so naive that they can't on occasion accuse their mother or father of unfairness or wrongness; by the teen-age years, some criticism and even waywardness is expected. Not so with Kathy. She was trusting, obedient, and in agreement with her Catholic family until shocked into disillusion by the realities of nursing.

Nurses see at first hand the suffering that belief systems of all sorts try to explain, correct, or justify. Kathy saw no possibility of justification. And she saw more: in any large hospital, there are mistakes and crass behavior that nurses in particular are powerless to prevent or even to remark upon publicly. Those in charge have no better a moral rationale for "who shall live and who shall die" than ordinary people do, yet those decisions are made on what seemed to Kathy a frighteningly ad hoc basis. She could no longer remain naively trusting of any figures of authority, including her parents, whose values she embodied.

Gradually, she became involved with liberal political and social causes of a less narrow scope than the "blind faith" of her parents. When she met Michael, he seemed to her to represent her new idealism and to offer her an escape into a better world. It might be said that this "love at first sight"—as sudden as a radical departure—was Kathy's first breaking away from her family.

Until that time, she explained about her growing disillusion with her parents, "I would never disagree with them; I was too unsure of myself." Michael gave her the strength to argue with them openly. Also, her parents' dislike of Michael and shock at their living together aided her rebellion and her separation. "When they had such strong antagonism to my falling in love and living with Michael," she remarked to me, "I more or less wrote them off."

At first, this trading off of union with idealized parents for union with an idolized husband worked. When the newlyweds first moved to New Orleans, Kathy was in a state of bliss. But she was not prepared for Michael's schedule as a resident in surgery. When he wasn't working at the hospital, he was on call and often summoned to Emergency. When Michael was off duty, he was so tired that he fell asleep instantly. Sexual union became infrequent.

Kathy might have maintained the pitch of involvement she required by getting work in an intensive care unit, but her preferred nursing assignment wasn't available. She tried to socialize with other resident doctors' wives, but accused them of being shallow and materialistic. There was no opportunity to cultivate the group adulation she had enjoyed among the nursing staff in Montreal, for she could find only fill-in shift work, impermanent and marred by anonymity.

Finally, she met Cindy, who had the sparkle of warmth and commitment Kathy sought. It wasn't even necessary for her to initiate the friendship; Cindy just came over to her and invited her to a picnic on the weekend. Kathy was delighted to accept, even though she was afraid of feeling out of place among a bunch of strangers.

At the picnic, she found just the opposite. It was if she'd known this large group for years. They were hospitable even to the point of hugging her. Cindy explained that these people were going to be crucial to the betterment of the world. They were part of the Divine Light Mission, and they were all devoted followers of the Maharaj Ji, the Indian guru, then based in the West. As Cindy pointed out to this politically aware young woman, even Rennie Davis, of anti–Vietnam War and Chicago Seven fame, was a member.

Kathy fell in love at first sight for the second time in a year. She was convinced that these people were sincere and dedicated, and that she could trust them even after such a short time. She couldn't wait to tell Michael and her parents that she was joining this religious group. She didn't know if they'd understand, but she really didn't care; she'd found a substitute for her family, her marriage, and her job, and an outlet for her idealism. Most of all, she felt she belonged with them.

Belonging is the ultimate seduction radical groups offer to those who join them. Without much of a self to inform them of who is doing what in their lives, radical departers are unaware that their own moves toward becoming separate individuals have provoked their discomfort. They are fraudulent because no one could possibly understand the "real me," although they are as baffled as anyone about who that person is. They are disillusioned because those they adulated have failed them, not because they themselves have severed such ties. They are worthless because no one needs them, although they are failing to meet others' needs. They feel lonely because they think they have been rejected, even though they are rejecting others.

Mental life is such that distinctions between what is happening internally and what emanates from the outside world are not easily distinguished unless there is a strong sense of self to mediate between the two. It's the self that does all that internal arguing and negotiating that we consider rationality. To the extent that these rash breakings away seem irrational, that is a measure of the lack of self these youngsters experience. To the extent that radical departers feel whole and genuine after joining, that is a measure of the belonging that, within radical groups, substitutes for an individual self.

A radical departer's initial encounter with the group he or she is about to join is only a first step in what amounts to a screening process that will sort out those who do belong from those who might be alien to the group. Although the screening process is not based on overt criteria, it is nevertheless similar to methods whereby any other sort of group assures that each new member will fit in well with other members, and that all of them will be relatively happy within the organization—in short, a series of meetings escalating to the mutual decision that the candidate is "right" for the group, and the group "right" for the candidate.

The first step in recruiting a new member is to approach a youth of about the same age and apparently of the same background as the members themselves. Young people "on the loose"—carrying a suitcase, bearing a backpack, looking bewildered or distressed—are special targets. For that reason, many groups frequent hotel lobbies, airports, and bus stations for the purpose of recruitment. An approach is more than simply handing out a leaflet or asking for a donation; the target of propaganda or solicitation may be anyone. Approaches are made only to a youth who appears interested, who asks a question, makes eye contact, or lingers longer than would an ordinary passer-by. That indication of interest is met with smiles and easy conversation in the manner, say, of freshmen during college orientation or of campers on their first day together.

There is rarely direct proselytizing at this point. Rather, the conversation drifts toward subjects of mutual interest—rehearsal for a play, as with Nancy Lewis, or the special beauty of the Wailing Wall, as with Philip Holtzman, or the pleasure of sun and song, as with Suzanne Marquette. Moreover, there is no probing that might be taken as judgmental. Those Children of God who failed to remark on Nancy's outrageous dress or to put down her request for marijuana are typical of the air of complete acceptance with which members approach a potential joiner. There is something very natural, a simple friendliness, in their approach, and it is especially disarming to potential joiners who feel so burdened with what they perceive to be the failings of an overcomplicated world.

How natural, then, that friendly conversation should lead to a spontaneous invitation to spend an evening with the group. Just as anyone, having struck up a conversation with a new neighbor and having discovered a mutual interest, might invite him to "drop over sometime." However, timing is more critical to this invitation, for group members are aware that a potential joiner is vulnerable right then, and may be less so at another time. Therefore the invitation to visit with the group is almost invariably for that same evening.

Only a small proportion accept the invitation. For every 1000 young people so approached, perhaps 250 are at a critical juncture in their lives. And of those 250, only 75 are willing to listen. Of those who stay to listen, a mere eight might feel so attracted to these new friends that they consent to the first visit. Many joiners have related to me a particular exchange that leads to their acceptance. They themselves initiate the exchange with some remark about the apparent happiness or calmness of the members they have just met. The members reply that it is like that all the time with them. The person must come and see for himself how they sing and eat together, and share their joy. Tonight . . .

For those who will join the group, that night is the most memorable of their lives. The bliss they have noticed in the few members who approached them is expressed by all the members as they welcome the visitor to their meeting place. Suzanne Marquette's first evening among the Moonies was "one of the most beautiful experiences of my life." She explained to me that "an overwhelming feeling overtakes you that you wish that somehow you could be like that. But no, you realize that there's not a chance in hell. But, maybe. And they say 'Why not?' and you say 'Why not?' " Philip Holtzman's first *Oneg Shabbat* at the yeshiva was a revelation to him. For the first time, he said, he saw "authentic, genuine people; no plastic there." Even Fred Vitelli, so crass and quick to criticize, was overwhelmed by the Armed Guard's "openness and honesty."

That night's get together—study group, party, Sabbath celebration, rehearsal, or ordinary evening—invariably includes food, music, and singing, sometimes dancing as well. The mood is often festive, but even when it is quite sober or studious in nature, the meeting is imbued with a spirit of camaraderie. All the members seem intent on making the visitor feel wanted, on convincing him that he is uncritically accepted, that he belongs. The potential joiner already "belongs," of course, in the sense that the members are the same age, share the same background, speak the same language. But like the best of hosts, members make special efforts to say how glad they are to have this visitor, to offer food, to include him in conversation, to smile, and often to hug or kiss him affectionately, as if they had known him forever.

In the course of this first introduction to the group, the prospective member begins to learn something of the belief system the group espouses. There may be explanations about their food, how pure or natural it is and why it is healthy. There may be prayers, or avid discussions about bringing peace, unity, and love to a torn and corrupted world. Still, this is proferred with eagerness to share—belief bubbles forth, of its own effervescence—and the visitor is free to drink it up or turn it down.

Many do turn down the offering. They feel uncomfortable amid this barrage of bliss and leave the meeting place relieved to get back to the usual world. This suits the group just fine. They have no interest in a young person who might have lukewarm sentiments toward the group.

Those who will ultimately stay are as smitten as any young person just fallen in love. Before the evening is out, about one in four of those who visit have either chosen to join on the spot, as did Philip Holtzman and Kathy O'Connor, or accepted a second assignation: to a retreat.

Again, this invitation may be withheld. Most radical groups are particularly wary of youngsters who may be runaways or who appear disturbed. They fear situations in which they might be accused of harboring a person against his will or to his detriment, and the lawsuits that could result. They look for the right "fit," and are careful to keep the relationship a voluntary one of mutual consent among "mature" individuals.

The retreat is usually held in a secluded, rural, and often strikingly beautiful spot away from the busy city that surrounds most groups' central meeting place. Here, members congregate not for the few hours of a meeting, but for at least a weekend and often longer. There is ordinarily no television or radio through which the outside world might impinge; telephones are scarce. It is as though there were no outside— no appointments to keep, hassles to endure, criticism to answer, or any worldly chores, schedules, deadlines, or expectations. For the visitor to a retreat, the ties that bind him to the world are severed; he is removed in many ways from realistic living.

With everyday concerns whipped out from under them, new visitors to a retreat tend at first to feel some anxiety. They don't know what to expect. Nancy Lewis had been warned by her friend Flo not to go, because the group sounded to Flo like a cult. Jamie Gould was aware that some of the people who had accepted the invitation to attend the Scientology meeting his first evening there refused to go to the retreat. Jennifer Green found herself in Taos, a city she didn't know, among strangers, all of whom knew each other, unable to participate in chatter about a therapeutic program with which she was totally unfamiliar.

But any anxiety is quickly dissipated. Retreats are a well-known tool of both secular and spiritual organizations for elevating the spirit and welding group solidarity. Participants are lightened of their burden of daily concerns and primed by the expectation of something "different" about to happen to them. The first hours are geared for unwinding. Good food is served and there is music, group singing, and shared ritual. Sheer "feelin' good" unites the members; they feel love for one another individually and a sense of loving union with the group as a whole. Talks begin, discussions, study, prayer, more ritual. And then prospective joiners, enthralled first by the medium of the happy people surrounding them, begin to listen to the message too.

Joiners have told me that during the retreat, the group's ideology, which seemed mere background noise to them before, suddenly makes immense sense to them. They feel a new clarity to their thoughts; the words they hear seem rich with significance and truth. Meaning dawns on them. This is the way the world is to be seen, this is the way in which to see ourselves. The intensity, sometimes euphoria, is so gripping that nearly half of those who attend that first retreat will decide to stay within the group.

Again, timing is important in this final screening step as the group embraces potential recruits. Should the retreat follow by more than a few days the first happy visit to the meeting place, it is doubtful that the visitor will actually show up at the retreat, even if he has enthusiastically accepted the invitation. Bliss, apparently, does not live long without feeding.

After a moving, "meaningful" retreat, about half choose to join. Would-be joiners seldom hesitate long in making their decision to stay within the group. Suzanne Marquette and Fred Vitelli did not leave the Unification Church and the Armed Guard at all after their retreats, and at most the joiners tarry on the fringe only a few days before declaring their choice to become members and informing their families of their decision.

Not all those who decide to stay stick out the first six months. Some are recalled into the world by other interests, or don't get along well with fellow members or with leaders, or simply can't maintain the sense of peace and happiness that at first moved them. Others who don't stay may never have intended to in the first place; they are fly-by-nighters looking for temporary shelter. For any 1,000 youngsters who are approached, the figures show that only one becomes a committed member who stays longer than half a year. The group is able to recognize from among potential recruits those who are most likely to become committed members, and would-be joiners only persist throughout the screening process if their belonging is likely to prove satisfying.

Satisfaction is putting mildly the feelings new joiners have related to me. Kathy O'Connor rapturously announced to me, "I'm really going to make a difference in this world." Jennifer Green, who "never knew what it was like to be at peace with yourself," said, "I've found it here." She called herself "a new person," and Dennis Ericson, echoing that sense of rebirth, said he was "a new man." "I feel so close to people now," he elaborated, "and I never did before."

These feelings of peace, love, and transcendence are, of course, what these young men and women had noticed about group members at the time of the approach, and it may be that members' expression of beatitude is a *sine qua non* of the potential joiner's original attraction to them.

But there is more to come as recruits continue through the screening process. Quite the opposite of perceiving the danger of these groups, as parents do, these young initiates perceive an absolute haven. Members reach out to comfort and to make comfortable a youngster who has been for some time frightened and in great discomfort. They are not only warm, but also protective. Parental fears to the contrary, recruits are never threatened with violence, are not seduced with drugs, and are not subjected to impulsive or destructive sexuality. To a girl like Nancy Lewis, already well over her head in promiscuous sex and drugs, the group may offer her protection that her family could not.

This safety is proferred to the new recruit in an atmosphere that seems devoid of pressure. Members appear not to compete with one another. Unlike peers in the outside world, there is no teasing; they do not vie to put one another down or show each other up. "I had friends before," Philip Holtzman explained, "but here we study together; we don't compete." For a child who may have received of late a steady stream of criticism at home, and certainly has been suffering relentless self-disparagement, uncritical acceptance comes as balm to a raw wound.

There are few demands related to the world at large that recruits are asked to live up to. Almost always, members dress alike in humble garments. A novice member need not worry about being in style or looking cool; no one has designer labels. They are all plain folk together, earthy, unacquisitive, disinterested in that materialistic show of possessions that, outside, stratifies and divides society. "Suddenly everything makes sense to me," Nancy claimed. "Money is meaningless, destructive."

And yet, though everyone is the same—a truly egalitarian society—to the new joiner these people his own age appear to be much wiser than he is. They know something he doesn't know; how else explain their bliss? They have the answers he himself has been unable to find. Indeed, the answers are written in texts he need only memorize—how simple—and are embodied in a single idea that seems very grand, or in the person of a leader upon whom these helpless-feeling youngsters can depend absolutely.

All this is especially emphasized to recruits during the first weeks of their joining, when they receive special instruction, help, and encouragement from senior members. New joiners are promised that they too will achieve wisdom and the peace that comes with it. "This is just the beginning," experienced members say to the recruit, who marvels at the joy of his first days among them. "You can be like us too; just wait and see."

And so, invaded by a benevolence he or she had never felt before, the new joiner drops a coin into the slot and calls home. Thus begins the belief and belonging of a radical departure.

4

Inside the Group

From the first weeks of their joining through a period of intense commitment that may last a year or even several years, radical departers appear extraordinarily similar to one another. Seeing these nine joiners two weeks after they broke away from their former lives, it could not have been guessed that, for example, Nancy Lewis had been filled with spite or that Ethan Browning had nervously immersed himself in a panoply of interests. Not one of them any longer experienced the self-doubt or exercised the entrenched defenses that had colored their previously distinctive personalities.

To a person, they and all joiners become suffused with self-confidence, a surety of righteousness that is absolutely impenetrable. Incredibly narrow dogmatism replaces free inquiry. Even those with the most analytic minds—Ethan, with his broad-ranging intellectualism, and Philip Holtzman, with his carefully academic intelligence—can no longer perceive the possibility of any view of the world but the one their group espouses.

They ride the crest of a flood of self-esteem, which they express in oceanic terms. They were "filled with love," everything was "beautiful, really, really beautiful," they were "significant in the universe." This self-esteem has a selfless quality about it. For example, none of these nine individuals boasted about accomplishments that were unique among their group, or measured themselves by comparison with other members. Their peculiarly impersonal self-esteem is derived from their belonging to a group whose beliefs serve a purpose beyond selfhood.

Committed members of these groups refer to their former selves before their departure as to a stranger they can barely recognize. Fred Vitelli talked about "that asshole" he had been as though it were someone else. Nancy could no longer understand why she had ever needed drugs or been attracted to the theater. Ethan felt that all his previous reading had been a sterile intellectual exercise; the Hare Krishna texts moved him deeply. In comparison with the present, the past and all the relationships they had had before their joining strike members as "plastic." Afterward, everything is "real." Kathy O'Connor was so astonished at this new feeling of authenticity that she "had to keep pinching myself" to test its permanence.

And they are happy. Most radical departers claim to be happy for the first time in their lives, or never to have known what real happiness was before. They say that they feel deeply excited, and yet have inner peace. To the beholder of their blandly radiant faces, this happiness is more beatitude than the sort of conviviality that would make one smile with them in shared good cheer, although their camaraderie with one another is touching.

This new "personality," always in astounding contrast to whatever personality they had shown before, is so uniform among members of radical groups as to make them nearly indistinguishable from one another. If there were no robe or uniform or cap to provide a clue, one would have to listen to the particulars of their relentless lectures on ideology to tell which group they had joined. Yet the groups themselves differ greatly from one another, and it is hard to grasp why a young man or woman would choose, say, the Children of God for a radical departure rather than one of the numerous established fundamentalist Christian sects that have become institutions. The underlying nature of the chosen groups and the outward similarity of their members shed light on what really happens to radical departers during their period of intense commitment, and why that is crucial to the future development of all joiners.

On the surface there is little resemblance between a time-honored yeshiva devoted to traditional religious study and the hostile mischief of a militaristic commune, or between the alien trappings of the Hare Krishna and the ordinary dress of the Healing Workshop. Several of the groups chosen for radical departure are not even radical within the context of their origins. Nothing is more respected than the yeshiva within its Orthodox Jewish community, or as revered in Tibet as the shaved heads and saffron robes of Buddhist monks, from whom the Hare Krishna adopts its dress.

Yet parents of joiners and society at large have little doubt that the groups these nine young people joined and hundreds of others loosely labeled "cults" are alike enough to be lumped together, whatever their origin. They are right. The mere fact that these groups are chosen as the focus for radical departure points to some underlying similarity.

The groups are chosen in the first place because of the double meaning they have to the youngster. Their "face value" is in keeping with whatever traditional values joiners' families hold. That's the face of the good little boy or girl doing what the family would wish. On the other hand, a group is not chosen unless there is a shared perception that it has placed itself outside society. While every group has affinities with some traditional system of belief—this or that religion or philosophy, this or that social ideal—none is in the mainstream of that system or is acknowledged by it. The group itself is aware of its exclusion, and counteracts it with its own vehement exclusivity. The original choice of a radical departure, then, is one that is bound to shock parents, and bound to strike their children as just what parents *should* approve.

However, the groups differ greatly in both their outward trappings and the nature of their beliefs. It would be impossible to make a list of characteristics that fit even these nine examples without numerous qualifications and exceptions. But just as a youngster chooses a group that provides a psychologically painless way to break away from parents, joiners stay with the group because its structure provides a psy-

chological haven that meets their particular needs at that particular time
in their lives. That structure and its appeal are easily noticed by following these nine joiners as they take up their new lives inside the
groups.

From the instant that Philip Holtzman committed himself to stay with
the yeshiva in Jerusalem, his life became almost antithetical to the life
he had led at home in Denver. Instead of the luxury he was accustomed to, he lived at subsistence level. His room was a tiny cell cut
into ancient stone in the Old City. In winter, especially, but even in
summer, the room was cold, dank, and dark. His bed was a canvas
cot, his bedding old, torn blankets. A new down-filled comforter sent
by his parents was turned over to the head rabbi to be donated to the
poor. There was a washbasin in one corner of this bedroom, but the
toilets and showers were several minutes' walk away.

His monkish cell was Phil's only privacy. "He cherished his privacy," Mrs. Holtzman remarked to me wistfully, but Phil didn't seek
to be alone at the yeshiva. The entire group of about 150 young men,
all from relatively affluent, educated, and only superficially religious
backgrounds, shared meals, services, and various rituals in unison. Like
his fellows, Phil preferred communal activity to the pleasures of soli-
tude he had once enjoyed.

There was, anyway, little time for any sort of self-indulgence. What
time was not devoted to bare necessities and to communal devotions
was spent in study. Traditional Jewish study is not easy. Orthodox Jewish training requires the memorization of long tracts of the Torah—
the first five books of the Old Testament—and of the Talmud, a com-
plex commentary on which Jewish civil law and religious observance
have historically been based. Phil spent many hours each day discuss-
ing fine points of interpretation and in a taxing form of debate, the
point of which was not to challenge the basis for belief, but to "get it
right" in all details. Even silent study was done in the company of a
partner, Zev, the blue-jeaned Canadian Phil had first met at the Wailing Wall.

Not only did Phil's joining deprive him of the wide-ranging liberal
arts subjects he had pursued at college, but many other former plea-

sures were now abjured. He had been politically active at the University of Colorado; there was no time now for "outside" activities. He had enjoyed popularity with both sexes at college and had been dating his girl, Marcie, for over a year. At the yeshiva, girls were not permitted to mingle with boys except on Friday and Saturday evenings, and then only under stringent supervision and regulations that forbid any touching, even of hands.

He deprived himself of extensive physical exercise. A star athlete in track and gymnastics at high school and the university, he had time only occasionally to work out with weights to keep his muscles toned. Nose-to-the-grindstone demands kept him bent over his books most of the time; he grew pale from many months of the scholar's indoor life.

Although youthful members of modern Israeli yeshivas no longer wear the long black caftans and broad-brimmed hats of tradition, there is a uniform of sorts. Phil had to cut his hair short over the skull and let his red curls grow over the ears to form long side locks. Beneath his street clothes he wore at all times a garment knotted at the corners for praying. A skullcap, called a "yarmulka" in his country and a "cipa" in Israel, was always on his head.

This general shunning of members' accustomed comforts and personal choices is typical of the groups radical departers join. The rich array of all sorts of foods, clothing, friendships, study, and entertainment offered in a middle-class environment is pared down to bare asceticism—and they welcome it.

The reason usually given by the joiners themselves for their adoption of a simple way of life is ideological. They shun materialism because it "corrupts," because acquisitiveness has led to inequities among people, or because only with utter simplicity can a person come to experience true love and inner peace.

This ideological rationale is valid as far as it goes. Shared simplicity is fundamental to the selfless aims of monastic orders in all ages, for both sexes, and in belief systems as various as Christianity and Hinduism. The most ordinary among us can appreciate how Spartan conditions can strip relationships to the basics during wartime or even on a vacation camping trip. But there must be more to it than that. Soldiers don't willingly go back to the deprivations they endured in order to preserve the intensity of friendship they experienced, and the most dedicated campers are glad to get back to their accustomed comforts after two weeks of the "natural" life. Yet Phil and many of the others cheerfully gave up creature comforts for well over a year with no longing at all for down quilts and pleasant bathrooms. Just as important in interpreting their flight into asceticism is the fact that hardly any of the joiners endure that way of life for more than two years. These are not young people with a religious vocation.

Youngsters from very intense religious backgrounds, in fact, seem exempt from radical departures. Fundamentalist Christians, for example, were never among these groups; sects in the fundamentalist Christian style, such as the Children of God, are made up mostly of members who have had the usual modicum of religious education in various traditional Protestant churches. The Israeli yeshivas I studied catered to Reform and Conservative Jews, not Orthodox ones. In groups styled after Oriental religions, a disproportionate number of the members are from Catholic and Jewish backgrounds, also with moderate or no commitment to their religion before their departure.

There are also general differences in how harsh deprivation is. Although radical departers without exception come from the middle class, those toward the lower end of the socioeconomic scale tend to opt for the most ascetic Christian-style groups while those accustomed to the greatest luxury tend to choose Eastern-style groups with the least deprivation. However, for every joiner, his choice results in a substantial lowering of living standards and a drastic narrowing of personal choice.

I think self-deprivation is a relief because of the multitude of strings that have been attached to luxury for these children, and that are now undone. First, there is the threat that if they are unalterably attached to the comforts their parents have bestowed on them, they will one day have to pay for comfort themselves. Frightened as joiners are of being unable to cope with the demands of adult life, a high standard of living is perceived as a burden. It was a real pleasure, not only to Phil, but to all these joiners to discover within themselves the resources to get along on very little from the outside world.

Second, every particular of deprivation is chosen for them. They don't have to decide, say, to sacrifice the purchase of a coveted record

album in order to have money to take their girl friends to a fancy res-
taurant. They don't become enmeshed in the tangle of family emotions that is often involved in the "free" choices offered teen-agers—
letting them choose their clothing and then criticizing their judgment,
encouraging the eating of healthy foods but disapproving of a vegetarian diet. In the yeshiva, food was what was set before Phil and his
fellow members. There was no possible hassle about hair style because
there was only one hair style, as there was only one course of study,
one time, place, and formula for doing everything from praying to
bathing. In every group, ambiguity is minimal. Every question has an
answer, every person has a duty, every hour has an assignment. There
are definite dos and don'ts, shoulds and shouldn'ts, either stated explicitly in the group's texts or in leaders' teachings or implicitly shaped
by group pressure. There are rules imposed for diet, dress, and de-
meanor. To parents who value independence, it is shocking to see their
children so ruled by conformity. They are sure only browbeating could
achieve this obedience. But browbeating isn't necessary; joiners gladly
trade in their autonomy for dependence.

Before joining, what strikes these young men and women as fateful
decisions—what "style" of person to be, what career to prepare for—
have weighed them down. After joining, these concerns evaporate. The
single decision to join may be momentous, but it is the only choice
the joiner has to make. The wonderfully light sense of a burden lifted
is nothing short of euphoric.

There are still other ways of looking at why deprivation is sought.
Many, if not all, joiners have been grappling with the impulsiveness
typical of their age, that pull to try out risky things, from driving fast
to sleeping around. Contrary to popular opinion, radical groups don't
encourage self-indulgence among their membership. Most religious sects
explicitly forbid drugs, and sex is allowed only in certain circumstances, usually marriage. Readers will recall the unprecedented mass
ceremony in Madison Square Garden in 1982 in which the Reverend
Sun Myung Moon married 2,075 barely acquainted couples of his
Unification Church, the Moonies that Suzanne Marquette chose to
join.

For supposedly autonomous middle-class children, this is certainly a height of self-abnegation. How these assigned sexual relationships will turn out is not yet known. Very few choose on their own to marry while in the group; many who were sexually active before their departure prefer abstinence after joining. I have not seen even one example of a marriage that continued after only one of the partners made a radical departure.

Kathy O'Connor is an example, not only of a failed marriage, but of the role of sexual abstinence. At first, her husband, Michael, was pleased that Kathy was involved with her new friend Cindy in a religious experience. He felt that with this outlet for her unfulfilled idealism, she would be happier in New Orleans. Within weeks, however, Kathy went from mere happiness to ecstasy and bliss. When she tried to share her excitement with Michael, he was incredulous. Her dramatic mood shift baffled him; there seemed something unreal in her euphoria. The more deeply involved she became, the more confused and angry Michael was. Finally he told Kathy she was either to leave the Divine Light Mission or she was to leave him. She moved into the Divine Light Mission ashram that night.

Kathy left sex as well. Although she had enjoyed an active and exuberant sex life with Michael even before her marriage (the obviousness of her sexuality had rankled her parents), she willingly gave up sexual activity after her radical departure. The group as a whole abstained from alcohol, drugs, tobacco, and meat, which "wholesome" freckle-faced Kathy, always concerned for her health, gratefully accepted.

Nancy Lewis, who had certainly risked herself physically and emotionally by heavy drug use and unchecked promiscuity, took no drugs whatsoever during her stay with the Children of God and no longer indulged in casual sexual relationships. The theater, with its overtones of a wicked and indulgent life, lost its appeal almost overnight, as though she had been waiting for a way to get out of her own somewhat scary fantasy before it could come true.

Jamie Gould, who had never experienced a settled relationship with a girl, fell in love with Julia, a fellow member of the Church of Scientology. Their relationship, marked at first by a shared zeal, survived their ultimate disillusion with Scientology beliefs and they eventually were married.

Nevertheless, one hears of scurrilous goings-on within some groups, and this is so occasionally. The Healing Workshop, the therapy group that Jennifer Green joined, tolerated considerable sexual involvement among members, but the pattern of it is telling. New recruits were under some pressure to become involved with senior members in usually monogamous relationships. Many women harbored secret and not-so-secret desires for Kurt, their charismatic, ginger-bearded leader. Beautiful Jennifer caught his eye, soon became a favorite, and was added to the group of women he slept with.

To Jennifer and to new female recruits who won a senior man's favor, these sexual arrangements were seen as protective, indeed fatherly, as though there were a great difference between the tough, uncaring sex they had experienced in the outside world (if they had had sex at all) and this safe alliance within the group. When a group fails either to forbid or to channel sexuality into specifically approved relationships among members—and I have seen a few "anything goes" communes—the results are disastrous for the individual involved and for the viability of the group.

Given the backgrounds of the joiners, one has to marvel at their self-control in so drastically and so suddenly curbing their pleasures. Yet they are bolstered by their own relief as they refind childhood supports and parental controls, and by several other aspects of the structure of radical departures. For example, they are distracted from their former fears and fantasies by incredibly demanding schedules to which all members conform.

Jennifer and the other members of the Healing Workshop were up by 6:00 A.M. for a routine of calisthenics. This was followed by a day-long round of "therapeutic" activities that included two long and intensive encounter groups, "co-counseling" sessions in which two people engaged in mutual psychotherapy, and confrontation sessions called "target time," in which behavior unacceptable to the group was exposed and attacked. The residents were also expected to read material by Arthur Janov, Fritz Perls, Abraham Maslow, William Shutz,

Eric Berne, and other literary heroes of the human-potential movement, as well as Kurt's own writings, mostly poetry. The members prepared their own health foods for every meal and cleaned up afterward in true communal fashion. There was a list of household chores, which rotated among members, and the same pertained to general upkeep of their rural property.

Kathy O'Connor also coped with a rigorous regime, that demanded by the Divine Light Mission: up at 5:00 A.M., asleep only by midnight. The day included many hours of meditation interspersed with religious services; the rest of the time was spent out on the streets selling Divine Light Mission Literature or recruiting new members. With no time to spare, Kathy gave up nursing.

Ethan Browning, at the age when parents know to expect lots of sleeping from their youngsters, slept only four hours a night and yet never felt tired. He had always studied hard and read a great deal in the sciences, philosophy, and history, as well as novels and newspapers. His mental energy and catholic taste were now directed to the tracts and tomes of the Hare Krishna sect alone. Whereas he had formerly found time for sailing, chess, flute performances, and debating, what time was left from study now went to keeping the large temple clean and doing kitchen work.

These hard and often rigid regimes have been accused of leaving members exhausted, so drained of energy by constant demands, exhortations, and scheduling as to appear zombielike. I have never seen a member who resembled a zombie during his or her period of commitment to the group. Quite the opposite; Ethan's report of never feeling tired even after a scant four hours of sleep each night is echoed by Jennifer, who said, "I used to be tired all the time, but I'm full of energy now. I eat well, I sleep well, and I don't agonize about myself or my life any more." Relieved of having to worry about the self they haven't yet found, group members appear vigorous, energized, and excited by their new capacity for work.

I think this is important. Children of middle-class families can't avoid knowing that they are not an economic necessity to their parents, as to either the labor or the earnings they might contribute. Indeed, they may be only too aware, as Nancy Lewis was when her parents dwelt on the money they had spent on her, of being a drain on family resources and of the nonmonetary return that is expected from parental investment. Every radical group, no matter what its persuasion, relies fundamentally on its membership for labor and for financial support.

For children who have tasted only the dregs of self-esteem, being needed lifts the spirit. They become suffused with self-confidence; their self-esteem fairly soars. This is all the more so in that they can hardly fail: the needs that must be met, while they may take many hours, are rarely difficult and are almost always done in company with others who share the chores.

Besides household chores and grounds maintenance in which members participate, the work is primarily directed at raising money to support the group and its leader, and recruiting, which indirectly supplies both more labor and a broader financial base. Some groups send their members out onto the streets to beg for money from passersby, sometimes under the guise of asking for donations to a cause or to a euphemistically named front organization rather than in the name of the group itself.

More frequently, money-raising is legitimized by the sale of literature. Some groups run businesses of their own staffed by members; a few expect members to work at some outside job not connected with the group. All expect earnings to be turned over to the commune, and it is not rare to request that personal possessions and cash resources also be donated, or a percentage of them, called a "tithe." Each of the joiners studied here participated in the economic support of his or her group in one way or another.

The Divine Light Mission to which Kathy belonged expected her to turn over her material possessions when she left Michael to live in the ashram. There each morning the ten ashram residents and other members who lived communally or alone outside the temple congregated to receive their daily work assignments. Everyone spent some amount of time selling Divine Light Mission literature, and all cash earnings were turned in to the ashram at the end of the day.

The Church of Scientology organized the selling of literature by establishing bookstores and other businesses. Jamie worked in one of them, spending many hours each day selling Scientology tracts by its leader, L. Ron Hubbard: *Dianetics: The Modern Science of Mental Health; Have You Lived Before This Life?* In addition to turning over the money from these sales to the organization, members paid for various courses of treatment that were to lift them to higher spiritual levels. Jamie spent thousands of dollars in an attempt to reach the stage of "clear" by being "audited" and "processed"—all Scientology terms. He used income from his ample trust fund to help his group further: $50,000 went to investment in an office-supply business to be run by the Church of Scientology.

This exorbitant amount of money seemed to Jamie well spent. He bristled with annoyance at my remark that the cost of "auditing" and "processing" seemed high in comparison to other forms of therapy. He was as sanguine about his investment in the office-supply business as his wealthy father might have been about a stock investment in the ordinary world. The difference was that "investment" is a misnomer in Jamie's case. He had no equity in any business that might result.

Fees for "services rendered" were the basic support of the Healing Workshop, to which Jennifer's parents paid a monthly sum for her therapy and residence. Kurt's ambitious plans also required donations from commune members. Although the property was owned outright by Kurt, he told members it was being "preserved for posterity," leaving them to infer that he had no personal financial interest in the real estate. This commune was to be the first of many "clones," as he liked to call them, to be established around the country. For this he needed money in addition to fees, and frequently asked members to give generously to further the cause.

The financial contribution of members is the subject of long meetings and serious concern for every group. Business meetings deal with income and expenditure, profit and loss, accounts receivable and payable. At times the meeting concentrates on how much money each individual has brought in that week through street peddling, solicitation, and tithes from new recruits. Occasionally the tone verges on the ideological and becomes uncomfortably directed toward individuals, since fund-raising is seen as vital to the group's spiritual, therapeutic, or political goals. In all fairness, the costs of supporting members is as pressing on these groups as on any that are responsible for room, board, clothing, and all other necessities. Sometimes a person who has not done well is merely urged on; sometimes he is berated, and once in a while he is threatened with expulsion. This was especially true for Nancy Lewis, who had previously complained that her father thought of everything as marketable, including her. In the Children of God each member's earnings from "litnessing"—their leader's seeming compression of the words "literature" and "witnessing"—were closely monitored and publicly discussed. Most of the groups, however, relegated less successful income earners to other tasks.

One would think that young idealists disillusioned with materialism would find all this niggling over account books demeaning, if not transparent. They do not. Like the properly raised middle-class children they are, members find work itself gratifying and the chance to measure themselves in dollars and cents worthy. At best, group economic endeavors really are very much in keeping with the work ethic they have been taught. "My father used to complain that kids these days have it too easy," Dennis Ericson once remarked to me. "You know, I think he was right."

3HO, Dennis's commune in Vancouver, did not support itself with any of the usual devices of enforced tithing, proselytizing, begging, or selling on street corners. The members worked at various business enterprises, which were surprisingly successful. Besides the *futon* shops, in one of which Dennis had originally been introduced to the group, 3HO ran a health-food dairy and a massage and exercise studio. They manufactured leather sandals that were very popular, and received tuition through public courses in meditation techniques, health, and love relationships. The group had also bought into a successful bakery, and it was there that Dennis, his robe's white sleeves turned up over his burly arms, worked long hours, often through the night, in front of a hot oven. He found the work deeply satisfying.

For those young men and women who have organizational, administrative, or business talents, there are opportunities to exercise them in much the way an enterprising youngster might in the outside world. Suzanne Marquette, who, between the discipline of ice-skating and the volunteer work she had done in her former Minneapolis neighborhood, was more experienced than the typical young joiner, rose through the Unification Church organization by means of her skills. She started with a seven-day seminar at a rural Moonie commune near San Diego to learn their basic literature, liturgy, theory, and practice, and followed that by a twenty-one-day training program at a rural camp in northern California. She was soon made an assistant to the instructor because of the zeal and intelligence she showed, and within three months became an instructor herself.

She enjoyed getting up early, exercising with the new recruits, lecturing to them, overcoming their doubts. She recognized herself in some of them—wide-eyed innocents who approached this new experience with a show of promise and an air of trepidation. If she saw a new recruit wavering, she set herself the challenge of winning that particular individual over to the Reverend Moon's teachings. She was successful at this task, and it did not go unnoticed by her instructor and directors. If something had to be done responsibly and with enthusiasm, Suzanne would be asked. After five months, she was promoted to assistant director.

All of the talents Suzanne had used with such good result in the outside world she applied with a kind of disarming naturalness yet single-minded intensity. Always a high achiever, she continued to be productive within the Unification Church. The only difference between her former activities and those after her radical departure was the addition of a sense of purpose. "For the last couple of years," she told me when she had been among the Moonies for a year, "I can honestly say that I wasn't having any fun in anything I was doing. I was only going through the motions, although everyone thought I was having a ball. I fooled them. I even fooled myself sometimes. My Moonie life showed me just how meaningful life could really be."

Suzanne was also an excellent fund-raiser and recruiter. On recruitment detail, she would bring in three or four potential new joiners who couldn't help but be intrigued by the words of this winsome, pretty, and obviously sincere blond. On other work days, her sales of books and flowers and the donations she solicited brought in hundreds of dollars to further the work of the church.

Nevertheless, with the exception of 3HO's shops and seminars, one is struck by a certain juvenile quality in much of the work required of

radical group members. Selling flowers reminds one of raising money
for the sixth grade's annual trip to Washington, D.C., or selling cookies for the Scouts. There is a sort of playing at being grown up, which
is best typified, strangely enough, by the Armed Guard, the only one
of these nine radical groups to attempt serious interference with the
adult world.

Fred Vitelli and his fellow members of the Armed Guard didn't
live communally or have well-defined work routines. They lived in
separate apartments widely dispersed in Rome and worked at whatever
separate jobs they could find, donating money as needed to support
their various plans for political action. Meetings were held at least three
times a week at secret and rotating locations to which entry could be
obtained only through an elaborate system of code names, certain knocks
or numbers of telephone rings. The meetings were designed to keep
the group's morale up, to keep each other highly politicized, and to
plan their next target of attack.

Plans ranged from demonstrations to protest the presence of visiting dignitaries (usually American) and mass rallies in favor of nuclear
disarmament to sabotaging right-wing groups by cutting electrical wir-
ing or telephone cables. The Armed Guard occasionally planned more
violent adventures, including kidnapping, bombing, and killing. Although none of these most serious crimes came to fruition while Fred
was a member, the group was deadly serious. Their tension was palp-
able during meetings; there was much bantering among them to de-
fuse the fear children feel when contemplating dangerous games.

That Fred could find such frighteningly boyish goings-on deeply
gratifying is a measure of how psychologically young these joiners are,
and of the heights of naiveté their needs push them to. To a person,
members during their period of commitment remain oblivious to any
venal realities of their group.

The real business of some of these groups, when there is one, of
course goes on over the heads of the membership anyway. Some groups
bring in enormous sums of money, and although the membership is
encouraged to believe its earnings are used to further the ideological
goals of the movement, a great deal may be diverted from local communes to a central leadership. From headquarters, it goes to the set-

ting up of companies, capital expenditure, investment in stocks, bonds, real estate, and, too frequently, into conspicuous consumption for the self-aggrandizement of the leader. Like the Yogi Bahgwan of the Rajneesh Meditation Centers, with his fleet of twenty-eight Rolls-Royces, the Maharaj Ji of the Divine Light Mission had luxury cars and yachts on display at his mansion in Denver. Tax exemptions, now being successfully challenged by the courts, are claimed by such groups in their guise of religious institutions. L. Ron Hubbard, of Scientology, the Reverend Sun Myung Moon, of the Unification Church, and the Reverend David Berg, of the Children of God, have all been publicly accused of such misdeeds as fraud or income tax evasion, although even formal charges brought against leaders rarely result in conviction.

Not all radical groups are sullied by behind-the-scenes infringement of morals, ethics, and law. 3HO and its leader, Yogi Bhajan, an elderly Indian swami who lives in Los Angeles, is exemplary; yeshiva rabbis are almost always dedicated, honest individuals, and so is the leadership of other groups I have studied but have not described here. Nevertheless, rumors, scandal, and occasional criminal convictions are ubiquitous enough that one would think well-educated youngsters would harbor suspicions of being used. Again, they don't—and that suspension of nagging skepticism in favor of absolute faith is at the core of their experience while with the group, and is a source of their year or more of extraordinary happiness within it. Every single member, no matter how others may think he is being used and abused, believes in the higher cause that is to be served through his effort.

I have spent hundreds of hours reading the voluminous works of all the many ideological groups I've studied in my own effort to understand what their beliefs are, and why radical departers should be so moved by them. Their vocabulary is theological, political, or therapeutic, depending on the avowed nature of the group, but they all sound the same. They are replete with tautologies ("Being here as a group brings us together") and such everyday truisms ("Life can be difficult") as to be trite. Mostly they are incomprehensible to outsiders and, I suspect, to most members as well. But in a curious way, it doesn't matter. While verbal complexity enhances the apparent transcendency of the belief system, there is relief in not understanding, great comfort in knowing that there are those at the top who do indeed understand.

Also, it doesn't matter what the beliefs are, even if they were lucidly presented. So long as there is a match between the group's avowed ideals and those of the joiner's family, the "packaging" of words and rituals is beside the point. When Nancy Lewis joined the Children of God in 1975, there were two other sects—the Foundation Church and the Process Church—that would equally well have echoed the Methodist Sunday school of her childhood, even though the tracts they followed appeared to say quite different things.

Beneath the verbiage there inevitably lie the goals all mankind has always wished for—peace and unity—but the rationale for achieving those goals is lost somewhere in an almost purposeful anti-intellectualism, or, at times, perfect nonsense.

When I asked any of these radiant youngsters the root of their happiness during their most committed phase, they unhesitatingly answered in memorized ideological terms. Fred said, "We are going to wipe out imperialist injustice." Kathy responded with, "The Guru Maharaj Ji's message will spread throughout the world; there will be a New Age dawning." Ethan parroted the litany of the Hare Krishna, talking about the "sweet Lord" and loving everybody. Jennifer was "getting in touch with my true feelings."

As in any group in any field, certain jargon becomes commonly used by all members. Sometimes the jargon is comprised of entirely new words. Jamie, as a novice member of the Church of Scientology, was a "preclear." He could become "clear" (psychologically rid) of "engrams" (early unconscious conflicts) by "auditing" (counseling) and other forms of "processing" (therapy). There are many more pseudo-scientific terms in this commingling of religiosity, futurism, and psychology. But Jamie was transfixed. He found the jargon exciting and the writings of L. Ron Hubbard redolent with meaning.

In the Divine Light Mission, the word "knowledge" takes on a different meaning from the usual one—it refers to a certain ceremonial attainment of a higher level of consciousness and closeness with God—and this using of publicly understood language for private or idiosyncratic messages is also common. Unique use of language enhances group cohesion. Those who speak it are insiders; it cannot be understood by outsiders. This is reminiscent of children, who often wish to speak at least a Pig Latin that will baffle their elders and fortify themselves, although these members' avowed goal is for all mankind to "see the light."

Fortifying themselves by mystifying outsiders is only one aspect of the garrison mentality that afflicts many of these belief systems. Society has used the word "cult" pejoratively for all these groups, but to each group, only the others are described by that four-letter word. They themselves are the true product; the others are ersatz, exploitive, corrupt, or dangerous.

Phil's yeshiva considered all other forms of Judaism, including the form in which he had been raised, to be heresies. At one point he described his parents to me as infidels and heathens—acceptable epithets among the particularly zealot-ridden membership of his yeshiva. The head rabbi himself would not have used those words.

The outside world is generally considered to be not simply misguided, but bent on evil—particularly toward the group itself, which is therefore able to put down rumor or media coverage of misdeeds among its leadership as sinful scandalmongering. Members are frequently warned of what can befall them outside the protection of the group, sometimes in an abstract sense—the wages of sin—but often the threat is made personal.

Kathy was warned by the Divine Light Mission that her parents would try to convince her to leave, that they represented the evil of the world and might resort to lying, kidnapping, and deprograming. Her companions in the ashram said her mother and father were sinners, that they were spreading lies about the Maharaj Ji in order to discredit him with his enemies. The bottom line was that Kathy should rid herself of her parents entirely.

Nancy could see that the Children of God weren't trusted by those outside it, but accepted her mentor's word that this was due to sin, ignorance, and envy. More difficult for her to comprehend was actual animosity shown toward her, her friends, and her leaders when abroad in the streets. She herself could find nothing provocative in the Reverend David "Moses" Berg's writings, although *Mo's Letters* advised female members to frequent discotheques and singles bars in order sexually to entice potential new members. He called the method "flirty fishing"; its practitioners were "happy hookers in Christ." This appalling affront to the outside world was justified by the odd logic that stamping out sin was what all right-thinking people should be doing. Uncle Mo's version of a Child of God's mission went further still: "Systemites," outsiders who doubted God's or Berg's words, were manipulated by the Devil, and if they couldn't be persuaded, certainly they had to be stamped out.

Although Nancy was never asked to go "flirty fishing," it is telling that she enjoyed confrontation with her group's enemies; the garrison mentality welds the group together in the exultation of common victimhood. Suzanne at the zenith of her zeal also met even my mild questions with streams of propaganda, defending the fort of the Unification Church even in the absence of attack. Not all the radical groups I studied were so quick on the trigger, but in general these belief systems incorporate a them-against-us mentality. Young joiners' original perception that they were psychologically unsafe prior to their radical departure is now translated into a conviction that they are morally (sometimes physically) unsafe outside the group.

A garrison mentality is made possible when those inside the fort believe they, and only they, are witness to the Truth. Unique vocabulary and ringing jargon furthers these youngsters' sense that they are privy to momentous revelations.

All of the groups have an implicit or explicit premise upon which membership is based: a future-oriented achievement of some major personal, group, or, more usually, societal improvement that—if only everyone could see the light—would lead to their general aims of peace and unity. In the religious sects, the achievement might be salvation in a life hereafter; in a therapeutic group, "self-realization," "self-actualization," or the attainment of a conflict-free psychological state; political groups might be planning for the evolution or imposition of some new social order.

Believing itself brings immediate gratification. Questions are answered; certainty replaces anxiety. But ideology would not be enough if there were no ultimate payoff. Rennie Davis once told me with fervent enthusiasm of the New World that will come when the Maharaj Ji spreads his word to the masses. Kathy, whose joining has to some extent been inspired by the fact that so famous a protester as Rennie Davis was also a member of the Maharaj Ji's Divine Light Mission, told me that she felt committed to something "really significant in the universe." She was a part, a small one, but a part nonetheless, of a spiritual movement that was going to revolutionize the world. The Ten Commandments would finally become a reality. And her new way of life—her prayers and rituals, her diet—was a part of this grand scheme. As to the failure of Kathy's marriage, which should have been devastating to this young woman who had risked her parents' enmity by living with and then marrying a man outside her faith, "of course it bothered me when we split, but it really was for the best. Michael was obviously jealous. He couldn't understand how beautiful my life had become—how really, really beautiful."

Fred was even able to suspend obscenity and anger in explaining to me how he felt when he was infused with the belief system of the Armed Guard: "I used to be fed up with everyone, with the whole world. These people have taught me how to change that world. I don't feel angry any more. We have a serious mission here."

Dennis said, "I feel like I have a purpose here [in the 3HO], and that's different from how I felt before—ever before. I never felt good about myself out there. I used to dream about excitement or adventure as the answer to my problems; never something like this. It sounds stupid, I know, but I feel that I'm full of love now."

All the members I've interviewed were similarly convinced that what they were engaged in made sense not only for themselves in the present, but also for generations in the future. Yet when I probed further for what that sense was—since I had found so many of the tracts they were relying on so incomprehensible—I found that few of the members had a firm grasp on what these beliefs were about.

To me, this smacks again of the innocence of early childhood, when, in union with one's parents, who need not be understood in order to be trusted utterly, prayers are answered and all endings are happy ones. These young men and women do not want, nor are they offered, the chance to apply intellectual analysis to their belief systems. They simply want someone to tell them that if they are good—learn what they are asked to and do as they are told—they will be taken care of and everything will turn out all right. Uniform interpretation of doctrine is the rule, even when the way to achieve uniformity is ritualized in argument. In Phil's yeshiva much of the time was set aside to argue the derivation and application of the Talmud. And yet if disagreement went on too long in the classroom a kind of "closure" was invoked, and the "right" conclusion was accepted.

Not that a great deal of time isn't spent in readings, lectures, and recitals of the groups' belief system. In religious sects, the beliefs are further expressed in prayer, rituals, chanting, meditations, and exhortations from the leaders. All members are expected to study the teachings of their leaders, and together they discuss interpretation and plan ways to spread the word or to accomplish the avowed goals. Members are reassured by the illusion of freewheeling discussion, though to an outsider it would seem a charade of analysis that was more symbolic than substantive. As Nancy put it, "Frankly, a lot of what I read confused me totally." She added, "What really excited me were my new friends."

My interviewing of joiners was like peeling the layers off an onion. Beneath skin after skin of belief I inevitably came to a layer of belonging that I think is very close to the heart of a radical departure. Friendship, acceptance, a sense of total oneness with the group are each a *sine qua non* for the radical departer.

Nancy Lewis lived a nomadic life during her period of intense commitment. After her indoctrination in Fort Lauderdale, she lived in Children of God communes in Texas, California, British Columbia, and, finally, Philadelphia. "I must have met hundreds of guys and girls. They were all so refreshing, so wholesome." Jamie Gould, though struggling valiantly to understand the novel pseudoscientific lingo of Scientology, felt that his own grasp of the subject didn't really matter. His gut feeling about its inherent goodness was shared by so many like-minded friends within the group. Dennis Ericson told me that never in his wildest dreams had he ever imagined he could be living as he was in 3HO. His gentle friends contrasted strongly with the right-wing militarism of his father and with the angry rhetoric of the draft dodgers with whom he had undergone the arduous experience of the New Left's underground railway to Vancouver. Dennis became a teacher of 3HO doctrine, but it was to him an avenue to loving friendship, with its promise of serenity. He really was serene.

Those who apparently had had no dearth of friendships before their joining nevertheless detected a difference. Philip Holtzman, always a popular boy, informed me that he had "no plans to leave the yeshiva; it's my only home now. Before, I was leading an empty life, a meaningless existence. These are my only true friends; the others were plastic, unreal." Even Fred Vitelli, superciliously rejecting of friendship prior to his departure, felt himself to be part of a close-knit group of friends. "These people," he confided, "are the first ones I've met who are genuinely interested in making a new world where we can all live together as brothers and sisters."

Those on the outside can barely appreciate the intensity of communion experienced by these large groups of close friends. Their sharing of every aspect of their daily lives welds them into what can only be called a "group self." They are a unity almost by definition, since they are all doing the same things, holding the same beliefs, speaking the same phrases, wearing the same clothes, eating the same food, and working for the same cause.

Instead of integrating their various failings into their sense of the kind of person they are—the imperfect self that most adolescents come to terms with—radical departers leave self-doubt outside the door as though it were so much baggage. For the period of their commitment, these children give up the struggle to formulate an independent self and participate with relief and joy in a group self that, to them, has no flaws at all.

But this is by no means a complete retreat from the battleground of growing up. They have taken a giant step: the group self is vehemently *not* bound up with that of parents. Separation has begun.

For these children, however, separation can be accomplished only within the safety of joining. Or perhaps *re*joining is a better word, for their groups are built along the lines of an exaggerated and idealized family. For example, careful attention is given to serving "good" food. The definition of what is good varies, so that to one group "pollution" of food is assiduously avoided by using only natural products, or a vegetarian diet may be considered the only "clean" nourishment, or very hearty meals in which meat is eaten with gusto has the meaning of goodness for a group. The point is that the emphasis on food echoes closely a mother's care in assuring that her children have what she considers a wholesome diet.

Health in general is high on the list of important concerns in most groups, who prescribe calisthenics, regular hours, and "pure" habits in an effort to assure healthy minds and bodies. In fact, my studies revealed a bunch of unusually healthy youngsters. There was a notable absence of even the usual psychosomatic complaints, from the lack of energy to the bowel problems and headaches, that plague even this robust age group. Many groups take great effort to clothe their members neatly and to instill standards of hygiene. Dennis was always immaculately clad in the white robe and turban of his 3HO commune, and Ethan Browning took special delight in the cleanly shaven head and fresh yellow robe of the Hare Krishna. The ashes with which members streak their faces from forehead to the tip of the nose—and which might have seemed dirty around the Browning dinner table— had the meaning of purity. The Armed Guard's "uniform" stressed studied elegance as well as careful grooming. Fred Vitelli and his companions, antimaterialistic philosophy to the contrary, sported Gucci loafers and leather jackets, not styled after either the "leather scene" or the motorcycle-tough crowd, but more on the order of buttery suede of continental cut.

Every group has a place it considers home, whether the members all live there or only some use it as a residence, or even if it is used primarily as a meeting place. Some are elaborate; most are sparse and simple. Kathy O'Connor's Divine Light Mission ashram in New Orleans was a small wood-frame house in the university area. It was somewhat run-down, but kept very clean. Jennifer Green lived in one of four adobe buildings on the Healing Workshop's desert acreage. In California style, these residences were filled with plants and made comfortable with an abundance of mattresses and pillows, used, I'm pleased to report, for resting as well as for smashing. There was a hot tub and a sauna for the members' use. Political groups tend reassuringly to strew their meeting places with familiar treatises, leaflets, and propaganda posters. Even when members live spread out, as in the Armed Guard, their various living quarters are supplied with the same literature and posters, and furniture is usually as sparse and serviceable as in an office.

When there are many units within an organization, each commune is furnished like the others. Ethan moved from his Hare Krishna temple in Boston to one in Los Angeles and felt immediately "at home." The altar was draped in the same colorful lengths of cloth; the spare furnishings were indistinguishable from those in Boston; offerings of flowers in small vases stood beneath the familiar portrait of their Lord, Krishna.

The structure of relationships inside the group is also like a family's. The children—the novice members—share intensely in the way of brothers and sisters. They are "deprived," as all children are deprived, of the power and of the possessions of adults. Like children too, they don't really understand the preaching of their elders, although they feel the importance of it passionately. Their comfort in finding that there are people "above" who can provide answers to any questions is curious only if you think of these joiners as adults themselves; it's not at all strange if you think of them as children.

At the head of this family stands the central leader, the one with the ultimate answers. He is always a man, sometimes one with pretensions of benevolence, like the Reverend Berg, who preferred to be Uncle Mo to his "families," as he called his groups, but often as remote as a patriarch. Indeed, the deified leader of the Hare Krishna has been dead for 2,000 years. Charisma is a common ingredient, but not universal. When the Maharaj Ji was at the height of public visibility as leader of the Divine Light Mission, he was a chubby-faced 16-year-old in whose countenance, and in whose utterings, one could only by a leap of truly creative faith have found charisma.

Leaders do not even have to be well behaved to be revered. Nobody seems to know where L. Ron Hubbard, the leader of the Church of Scientology, has been since he was publicly accused of fraud and misrepresentation by former members and one of his own sons. The Reverend Berg, of the Children of God, is also missing since similar charges were leveled against him. The Reverend Moon, of the Unification Church, has been convicted of tax evasion. The Maharaj Ji's mother's mind-boggling shifts in favoritism between her sons must stand as a low-water mark in family relations, yet many members survived the storm to revere the older brother as they had the younger one. It is as hard to explain why such failings don't matter to members as it is hard to explain why 6-year-olds boast about their fathers no matter how inconsequential others find them.

The Healing Workshop's leader is typical of a living, present, and charismatic leader. When Jennifer fell in love with him, Kurt was 60 years old, burly, informal, but elegant. His ginger beard hinted at patriarchy. He had impeccable manners and was given to flowing phrases delivered with a vaguely foreign accent not readily placed, but attractive to the American ear. He was supposed to be a psychologist, but no one really knew. Fred's leader in the Armed Guard was a much younger version of a charismatic leader: Michel, an angry young man but dark, handsome, and seductively charming.

Whether the "father" of the group is absent or present, charismatic or boring, of impressive morals or an actual criminal, his "family" of boys and girls fantasize about him in the way of young children. The boys identify with him, attempting to adopt whatever they can discover of his pose, gait, and turns of speech. The girls wish to please and serve him.

An air of awe and reverence, sometimes actual deification and worship, is encouraged, especially in large groups made up of many units, by the customs of hanging the leader's portrait everywhere within the local home. Portraits of the Maharaj Ji, Kathy's "Perfect Master," were on just about every wall of her Divine Light Mission ashram: hanging from the balcony, smiling from the kitchen wall, even adorning the bathroom. There was a small altar and worship table surmounted by his image in the living room. Services there were led by the Maharaj Ji's representative and local leader of that unit, an elderly gentleman in a white toga who also lived in the temple.

Large organizations such as the Divine Light Mission, the Unification Church, and the Church of Scientology have headquarters where the central leader—if he is not "missing in action"—ordinarily spends his time. Since such organizations are also large businesses, there is a full executive and administrative staff as well as the leader's personal retinue, who may also have managerial responsibilities. Some among the central group constitute an inner circle of the leader's favorites. Members such as those described here, however, worship from afar and have no opportunity to know the leader of such vast groups at first hand.

A similar hierarchy exists within small groups such as the Healing Workshop and within each local unit of even the largest organizations. Suzanne Marquette's Moonie commune had a local leader who was definitely the person in authority, and even so small a group as Fred's Armed Guard, with no more than a score of members, revered their leader, Michel.

In groups of any size, and whether the leader is the only one or is one among a number of local representatives of the central leader, there is rather a scurry to become one of his favorites or at least to be close to the inner circle that surrounds him. The members of the inner circle act as teachers who represent the leader's beliefs. In the Armed Guard, the inner circle was made up of founding members; in the Divine Light Mission, it was comprised of members from India who had followed their leader to the United States in 1971; in 3HO, members could rise to high positions by virtue of a combination of seniority, zeal, and aptitude for leadership. Those in the inner circle—"elders," "senators," "lieutenants"—are one rank below the leader, closest to the seat of power without actually occupying it. When the members of the inner circle of a large group function as leaders of local units, as they often do, they may nevertheless exercise considerable power over the membership in their charge, and it is this secondary level of leadership that often sets the tone of a group. Even in Phil's yeshiva, where the chief rabbi was himself in residence, a handful of favored, zealous young rabbis was able to set the tone of harsh bigotry; the chief rabbi was a far more flexible, pragmatic sort of person.

Local or secondary leaders seldom climb beyond the inner circle to assume the central leadership of a radical group. Indeed, they get no public recognition for their success and usually out-orthodox the leader. They are truly defenders of the faith. Their master's adventurous or pragmatic spirit often enables him to enjoy independent thinking, while those in the echelon just beneath him tend to be hidebound conservatives threatened by change, and consequently rigidly doctrinaire purveyors of dogma. They might be thought of as permanent older brothers and sisters whose job it is to keep their younger siblings in line when the parents are not at home.

Below the patriarch and his elders, the hierarchy of the group is not much better defined than it is in a family, although the total membership may be in the thousands. Membership is typically divided into small units; Phil's yeshiva, with 150 members, was exceptionally large, Kathy's ashram commune of ten in the Divine Light Mission in New Orleans was unusually small. Groups of fifteen to twenty people living together are most common. Except for the leader and his chosen circle, all other members are called "novices," "trainees," "premis," "students," or other terms. Some may be considered "seniors" by virtue of the length of their stay. The juniors, however, make up the vast majority of the membership. Duties are assigned to them according to equitable rosters in most cases, but also by seniority, sex, and skill. New members are often given more of the "scut" work, but are also given most of the formal teaching and support from their elders or from senior members.

Rules and routines are imposed via edict from above or simply through group acceptance of their own traditional standards. But there are subtle rewards for adherence. The group itself warms to enthusiastic participation, and leaders reward good behavior with kindly words and smiles. There are often "graduations" from one level of spiritual attainment to the next or there might be a promotion to reward effort or special talent.

This was the basis of Suzanne's several promotions to positions of greater responsibility. Dennis was honored by being allowed to become a religious authority in his own right within 3HO, and his name was changed to Guru Sej Ram in recognition of his commitment to the higher calling of his group's healing mission. Phil, intellectually impressive in any context, was noticed by the young rabbis, who in turn mentioned this promising new member of the yeshiva to the head rabbi. Within a few months, he was given additional responsibilities, including helping to plan strategies for attracting new members and to curry favor in various government ministries from which some of the group's financial support was derived.

There is also overt or covert punishment for failure to comply and for displays of doubt and flagging enthusiasm. Verbal punishment ranges from mild criticism in private to painful attacks in front of the whole group. Shunning is also used, and can be either an extremely uncomfortable cold-shouldering and ostracism from group activities or more subtle ways of leaving the offending member out of the action. One can imagine the effectiveness of any degree of criticism on joiners who rely on unconditional acceptance.

Fred was the only one of these nine joiners who wasn't immediately sensitive to the particular form of criticism his group used to keep members in line. He kept waiting his turn to be called on to actually carry out plans discussed in the Armed Guard's secret meetings, but because he had entered the group through the back door of his love affair with Yvette rather than through ideological commitment, he remained suspect to the rest of the membership. In this deadly serious group, it was anathema to suggest casual outings for the sheer fun of a picnic or a swim, as Fred often did. Therefore, whereas he became convinced of his dedication to their shared mission, his comrades in arms never wholly trusted him and never did give him a responsible role in their more ambitious acts of political sabotage. He was slow to see the pattern.

A good deal of the self-regulation of radical groups is conducted in the course of their regular meetings, which, though nominally held for ideological purposes, inevitably overlap with personal ones. Much as the joiners I spoke with claimed that outer-directed ideological concerns had replaced their former focus on their own problems—allowed them to "get out of their own heads"—living communally proved to have its problems.

Many joiners have never lived away from their families, or have shared accommodation at most with two or three people. Now they are in groups of ten or more, living and working together twenty-four hours a day, week after week and month after month. Issues of privacy, space, noise, schedules, cleanliness, and neatness—mundane when compared to lofty ideals—take on immense importance in their day-to-day lives. Just as important are intense emotions generated by close-ness itself: love, sexuality, anger, jealousy. For example, Dennis and another young man in 3HO vied for the attention of a lovely girl, and they almost came to blows at one point early in his radical departure.

"Selfish" behavior and emotions may be kept to a minimum by the group's own willingness to subjugate personal desires to group goals and by the leader's imposition of restraint, but things do get out of hand. The "common good" is then reinforced through open com-plaint, discussion, and eventual resolution during group meetings.

When a group allows its ideological zeal to override its sense of community, interpersonal squabbles can escalate into explosive con-frontations that end with the expulsion of some members or even the dissolution of the group. The soothing over of dissension among members is vital to the survival of radical groups and to the mutual comfort of the members.

In a family, soothing of dissension is usually the special talent or province of the mother. A father may represent standards of conduct in an abstract sense, but when it comes to making each person com-fortable, mothers are traditionally the ones who are called upon to ar-range the concessions, compromises, and resolutions that will keep the family unified. That division of labor may be changing, but was cer-tainly typical of the families from which these nine joiners came, and of the middle-class families of radical departers in general. Yet strangely absent in the pseudo-family of radical groups is any individual who takes the part of the mother figure. Mrs. Moon exists, but she is kept behind the scenes and her role in "perfect parenting" of her group family doesn't include mothering. Instead, the group mothers itself.

This too cannot be an accident. In fact, the absence of a mother may be central to these children's effort to separate. Fathers, however important they are in so many other respects, are in these instances rarely the focus of separation. The information I have gleaned from these families hints that the fathers of many radical departers are, if anything, somewhat more remote from their children than is usual, and this may be reflected in joiners' preference for idealized, ideolog-ically oriented leaders rather than chummy ones. These children in many cases have fallen all the more deeply into intense identification with their mothers, or at least into longing for such closeness. Kathy O'Connor was named after her mother, Katherine, who was called "Kate" to distinguish between the two. The resemblance between mahogany-haired Jamie and Joanne Gould had often been remarked on. Ethan Browning's mother had lavished attention on her only child. Mrs. Green and Mrs. Marquette had intimately participated in their daughters' talents. The breaking away that such closely bound children must do in order to establish a separate identity and, often, one in alliance with their fathers is particularly difficult for them.

Group motherhood therefore kills two birds with one stone. Each individual member is separated from his or her actual mother and does not replace her even symbolically with a substitute figure. Instead, the group acts as its own mother, seeing to its own bodily and emotional welfare through all that concerned domestic care and soothing. Yet— and this is what makes giving up the actual mother possible—each individual finds in the group self the closeness and union that cannot yet be relinquished. He also finds the strength, the wisdom, and the concern for abstract ideological issues of the father he still needs and with whom he hopes to identify.

And so Phil, Nancy, Kathy, Suzanne, Jamie, Fred, Dennis, Jennifer, and Ethan found themselves, for the first time in a long time, unutterably happy. From a world in which they had been alienated, they entered a world where they belonged. Where previously they had experienced a spiritual void and cynicism, they now found belief. They had been useless, and here was work for them to do; worthless, and now they were saving the world. Impulses that had frightened them were now controlled. Choices too difficult for them to make had evaporated. In this strange never-never land of the radical departure, they participated in a group self by being individually selfless. They were both separated and united.

I gave a substantial number of these radical departers in their most committed phase standard psychological tests to see what relatively objective measures would show about their emotional state. The California Psychological Inventory, for example, measures the extent of psychological complaints. The Beck Anxiety Check List and the Beck

Depression Scale speak for themselves. On every measure, these young men and women seemed just fine, or at least no worse off than any comparable population of young men and women. Anxiety-related complaints—palpitations, sweating, tremor, diarrhea, insomnia—are seldom voiced. Depression-related ones—sadness, crying, self-denigration, lack of energy, loss of pleasure—are likewise rarely reported. They sleep well, their appetite is good, they feel confident, they worry less. There is an absence of feelings of guilt, of having wronged others. To the contrary, they have never before felt so confident and justified in what they were doing. It is this seeming calmness and equanimity that stuns frantic parents. Expecting fear and confusion, they often find self-assurance bordering on arrogance.

But they are not convinced that their children really are happy. Nor was Michael convinced of the genuineness of Kathy's euphoria. Nor were casual observers approached for donations by saffron-robed Ethan convinced of the authenticity of his bliss. Nor am I convinced that any of these radical departers are experiencing happiness in the way that most of us understand happiness.

First, it is all so sudden. One day a troubled youth feels empty, lonely, useless, sad, and cynical. The next day he overflows with ecstasy. Even falling in love is rarely so transforming, fraught as it is with nagging suspicions and of longings not quite fulfilled. One can't help but suspect something odd in this overnight transformation.

These youngsters' happiness is, in fact, peculiarly uncontagious. A therapist is ordinarily as easily caught up in another's joy as anyone—perhaps more so, since empathy is his stock in trade. But much as I have looked at beatific faces, heard gushes of apparent joy, understood intellectually what these joiners were saying about the peace and union they have achieved, something prevents me from being swept up by what I see, hear, and comprehend. Over and over, with hundreds of committed members of radical groups, I have felt that theirs is an "as if" performance, a case of bad acting in which the actor is himself carried away by the ringing truth of his role, yet fails to convince the audience.

Parents invariably doubt the sincerity of their child's performance. It is this air of spuriousness that may have led to the assumption that these children are brainwashed, or that they were "weird" in the first place. Although they have not been brainwashed, and certainly weren't weird, they are not quite whole either.

The "happy face" mask that joiners wear is uncontagious because it is not the whole face of their inner dynamics. One simply cannot shuck the brain cells that represent the entire predicament one was in in the first place. Conflict, fear, and hateful feelings may have the weight of useless baggage, but they can't be dumped outside the door of the mind. Unacceptable emotions can, however, be put temporarily into the cold storage of the unconscious while the child prepares, so to speak, more adequate mental shelf space on which they can be reorganized in time. Unconscious psychic reorganization is proceeding all during the time the child lives within his radical departure. Meanwhile, he forgets what has been stored. Of course his happy face seems blank to us; certain things are missing.

Suspicion that joiners' happiness isn't quite what it seems to be is confirmed by the fact that more than ninety percent of these children leave the group that has seemed to them to provide all the answers within about two years. During that time, when the life they espouse seems to them innocent and good, parents take their child's radical departure to be a rebellion. And it is.

5
From the Outside

A stunning fact about radical departures is that whereas the child feels benevolence and the group avows it, the parents respond to their child's leave-taking as to a slap in the face, and society in general sees the group as malignant. When an entity is perceived in such opposite ways, the tendency is to try to resolve the disagreement by discovering which is right. In this way of thinking, either the radical groups children join are as benign as the members inside say they feel, and adults are making a fuss over nothing, or they are really as hostile and damaging as outsiders think, and they should be done away with.

Psychiatrists are accustomed to thinking in another way. Any expression, they have learned over and over again, can have both a benign and a malignant meaning. Sometimes the person intends both messages but they are each to be understood by a different audience, as when one exaggeratedly compliments an individual's ostentatious outfit, hoping he will take it as a compliment but one's friends will see the built-in criticism. The double message can also be intended for a single recipient. A woman buys her sister a sweater as a present, though she knows it is a color her sister will never wear. Her benevolence is in giving the gift, her hostility is in making sure it is an ungratifying one.

Conscious uses of ambivalence directed toward others are, however, the exception. Far more often, ambivalent expression is unconscious and enables people to deceive themselves.

For example, a husband who is quite furious with his wife over some minor misdemeanor may forget his promise to call the plumber about the stopped-up kitchen drain. He, who loves and needs his wife very much, need not be aware of his anger; forgetfulness doesn't reflect on one's general good will. On the other hand, his wife may clearly see the hostility behind this piece of everyday sabotage and accuse him of ruining her day on purpose. Both are right. He doesn't feel angry; she has been the target of his anger.

Through long experience with radical departures, I have come to believe that both the "senders," who experience their message as kindly, and the "receivers," who experience that same message as hostile, are right. These children, so bound to their parents that they have been unable to separate from them in the gradual way of most adolescents, can break away from them only in a form that disguises their purpose from themselves.

Therefore, a child's experience of his departure into and inside a group and the parents' experience of the departure from their vantage point in the outside world are entirely different, although they are heads and tails of the same coin. While children are busy at their bliss, parents are nearly paralyzed by one of the most painful crises that can befall a family. But the work of both generations is directed toward the separation that eventually is the coinage of the more mature relationship both are seeking.

For the period of a radical departure, the work falls mostly to parents. Whereas their sons and daughters have narrowed their vision in self-protection, parents suffer a side-angle view. Joiners feel safe; parents appreciate the danger they are in. And whereas members have shelved painful emotions, their mothers and fathers are in agony. How the work proceeds and whether the family can come to terms with what their child has done to a large extent determine the outcome of a radical departure.

Until the phone rang in the Marquette home the Monday of Suzanne's radical departure, everything had been as usual. Peter Marquette had hurried through two cups of coffee and gone to work at his printing-plant office. Barbara Marquette was finishing some correspondence and paying bills, to get such nuisance work out of the way in time to pick up Suzanne at the airport. Her twin sons had left by car pool and were at nursery school. Her mind had just wandered to the prospect of perhaps baking something special to welcome her daughter back from the ice-show audition in Santa Monica when the phone rang. The call wasn't unexpected; Suzanne was to have reported the results of the audition before boarding her flight. At first, noticing that the familiar voice sounded somewhat strained, Mrs. Marquette thought that Suzanne might have had to change her flight or had lost her wallet—the ordinary fussy concerns a mother has when her daughter is far from home. When Suzanne followed the news of her successful audition by mildly announcing her decision to become a Moonie, her mother's reaction was blank shock.

Parents literally do not believe their ears. Perhaps it is a joke? But their child sounds dead serious. They ask for a repetition in case they heard the words wrong. Their child repeats the announcement. As if in an anxiety dream in which everything is heavy, clumsy, can't be made to work right, the voice at the other end of the line, this loved child, dumps words like "peace" and "happiness" as obstacles in the way of a parent trying to surface through a thickness of fear.

This bland quagmire is not manipulable. When parents find their voice—"Are you all right?," "Who has done this to you?," "Please come home"—the child is simply unmoved. Of course, she was all right, Suzanne reported. No one had done anything to her; she would not come home.

This is a crisis that has no precedent. When a person hears of the death of a loved one, the diagnosis of a serious disease, the fact of financial bankruptcy, these are all tragedies that happen to other people too. There are customs and institutions that are the know-how of life's ordinary crises; there are, at least, things that must be done and can be done. There are no bodies of knowledge, no customs or institutions, and few fellow sufferers to guide a family that has just suffered a radical departure. What's more, there really is nothing that can be done.

Emotional shock overcomes parents. They are paralyzed by indecision because there are no decisions to make. They are overwhelmed by chaotic sensations or numb from overload. It can't be true. Yes, the truth is eerie. Ethan Browning is sweeping the temple floor, Nancy Lewis is on her knees praying aloud to Uncle Mo, Dennis Ericson has dressed in white, Suzanne Marquette is soliciting donations and members on a street corner. These children are changelings.

A sense of eeriness is parents' front-line defense, a way of denying that this is happening in the real world of two cups of coffee and plans to bake dessert. By the time Mr. Marquette received the news from his wife and returned home, the next line of defense was in place: Suzanne was "not herself," to be sure, but there was a real-world explanation. She had been kidnapped, seduced, brainwashed, or was undergoing a nervous breakdown. Most of the parents I've spoken to have feared—and, I think, hoped—that coercion or illness was behind their child's radical departure. The Holtzmans were so convinced that Phil had become schizophrenic that they begged to see for themselves, but he refused to let them.

Were there fear in these children's long-distance voices, or even a monotonous passivity, such beliefs might endure. But the fact is that the more they speak to their absent children or read their letters over the next weeks, the more smug their children seem to be. They are opaquely happy, they know all the answers; it is their parents who have been duped and are to be pitied.

A third defensive ditch is dug: God knows what might happen to the child among those weirdos. The nine typical case histories followed here don't support the popular notion that awful things happen to members of radical groups. But no one can guarantee that the safety joiners seek is what they get. Media cult spectaculars come to mind: the Manson murders, the Jonestown mass suicide, Patty Hearst's indictment for bank robbery, the accidental explosion that killed Green-wich Village terrorists as they manufactured bombs. Some of these fears are real. Kurt, of the Healing Workshop, sexually exploited Jennifer Green and other female members of his commune. The Children of God to which Nancy Lewis belonged could be cruelly repressive of nonconforming members. Fred Vitelli's Armed Guard manufactured bombs.

All the members are, moreover, in a psychological state their parents don't recognize. "He was just acting very strangely, very different from before," Jack Ericson said of Dennis after several phone calls from the 3HO in Vancouver, "using words in a new way; and full of this love and peace horseshit. It just wasn't Dennis." Although parents lack more substantial evidence that anything terrible is happening to their child in the first weeks of membership, they may become awash with unprovable fears and determined to find out the truth.

Jennifer's mother did just that. Linda Green had called her local mental-health association for information about the Healing Work-shop even before Jennifer's visit to its Taos commune, but could find out nothing about it. After Jennifer's decision to stay with the group, Mrs. Green launched one of the most thorough research programs I have known a parent to conduct. She spoke with Jennifer's friends, with what few parents of current radical departers she could locate, and with former joiners who had returned home. She consulted the police, the courts, lawyers, and deprogramers. She read every article and book on the subject of cults, watched every television program and listened to every interview that could possibly tell her anything about radical groups in general or the Healing Workshop specifically. She read on the subject of brainwashing, followed up rumors about "mind-controlling" diets, and learned everything there was to know about the financial scams, sexual exploits, and run-ins with the law of group leaders.

These frantic efforts to know what's going on are very frustrating. For every large and well-known group, such as the Unification Church, about which a good deal is public information, there are hundreds of smaller groups, like the Healing Workshop, about which little is known. Mrs. Green might have felt on more solid ground if her daughter had, like Suzanne, joined the notorious Moonies, but still she would have been none the wiser about the particular unit of that large organization. The character of each unit varies with its leader, its membership, and the pressures the group bears. There is no way to tell whether an innocuous group will become more sinister over time, as was the case with the People's Temple when, under investigation in Guyana, its leader, Jim Jones, became increasingly paranoid and its members increasingly panicky. Finally, what one child finds devastating another can bear. While Kathy O'Connor was badly affected by disturbances within the Divine Light Mission, Jamie Gould, in the Church of Scientology, escaped a similar scandal concerning his group's leadership quite unscathed.

Unless the police or the courts are poised to move in on a group that has actually broken the law—the Healing Workshop, with its voluntary tuition, residence, and therapeutic program, was certainly not one of them—public agencies are no help. At 19, Jennifer was of consenting age even if Mrs. Green had known for a fact that Kurt had seduced her. As a minor, Ethan could have been considered a runaway, and could therefore have been placed under court control. By doing that, however, parents relinquish their own control. They are wisely hesitant to take so drastic a step with a child who hasn't been a chronic discipline problem, and are also reluctant to endure exposing their personal tragedy to the judiciary. Legal recourse doesn't resolve the dilemma that has led to this radical departure anyhow, nor does it prevent a repetition.

Parents who rely somewhat less on knowledge as a defense don't go to the lengths that Mrs. Green did, but they at least attempt to use the institutions, formal and informal, that traditionally stand ready to help a family in trouble. Sam and Ellen Holtzman went to their rabbi. Their synagogue had for many years run a program that placed children with families in kibbutzim, rural agricultural communes in Israel, for just the sort of inspirational experience they would have wanted for Phil and that he ironically exaggerated for his own purposes. The rabbi knew nothing about radical departures, and had nothing to offer but commiseration. The same was true of the minister of the Brownings' Episcopal church and the O'Connors' Catholic priest.

Several families sought out therapists who might have special knowledge of radical departures. There are almost no practitioners who have direct experience with joiners, but there is no end of theories, and parents are offered a full bag of conflicting prescriptions. "We didn't know where to turn," Lillian Lewis told me after Nancy's departure, "but we sure turned. We phoned everybody we knew or heard of; any hint of an expert was enough for us. We listened to and considered all alternatives: to leave her alone, or show her love, or give her hell, or deprogram her. We heard it all and got more and more confused. In the meantime, we didn't even have time to notice that our lives were falling apart."

The first period after a radical departure on the home front is characterized by the parents' almost total preoccupation with their son or daughter in the group. They eat, drink, and sleep their quandary. Many of the parents I have worked with withdrew from friends; the belief that something was wrong with these joiners in the first place, and the general opprobrium in which their groups are held, may make the event seem too humiliating to expose and discuss. The Holtzmans' many cultural interests lay unattended. The Brownings' focal dinners deteriorated. A pall of tension and irrationality fell over even as cheerful a household as the O'Connors'. Parents can't give their other children or each other the kind of nurture, support, and stimulation they have been accustomed to. How was Mrs. Marquette to explain to her four-year-olds that Suzanne was a Moonie when they nagged about ice-skating lessons from their big sister? The entire family is shaken to its very foundation.

Rarely can parents agree on a shared attitude with which to approach their rebelling child. The Marquettes are typical. Barbara, cake baker that she was, hoped to conquer by kindness over the long run. As the months passed, she began to send Suzanne "care packages," as though the Moonie commune were a freshman dormitory, with the difference that these offerings contained no confections or expensive delicacies that might affront. Rather, she listened to Suzanne's harangues on diet and stuck to carrot bread and unroasted nuts. She wrote newsy letters about the twins—they had turned five and entered kindergarten shortly after Suzanne's departure—carefully ignoring the far less tactful letters she received in answer.

Peter fumed. He took a frontal-attack position—by telephone, not letter—and hung on like a bulldog. He seemed not to realize that at the other end of the wire his daughter stood surrounded by devoted eavesdroppers ready to console her and justify their group's beliefs the moment her father hung up. Letters at least can be private. Eighteen months passed before Mr. Marquette agreed to stop shouting at his daughter.

Sometimes one parent, as often the father as the mother, becomes obsessed with punishing and eradicating radical groups in general in order to protect their child and the whole of society. They may join forces with equally obsessed individuals in a crusading mission altogether as single-minded and consuming as the belief their own child is experiencing. Other members of the family feel left out, neglected, and friends become frankly bored.

Stuart Browning, Ethan's father and a citizen of some weight in the Episcopal church and in Boston's business community, was instrumental in expanding a previously loosely organized band of anticult activists. He located a psychiatrist willing to lend clinical credibility to their effort, raised donations for their support, hired detectives to investigate possible abuses within the Hare Krishna and similar groups in the Boston area, and used his connections to make sure their findings received media attention. Eventually, these vigilantes established a referral system whereby parents of radical departers are put in touch with deprogramers throughout the New England area.

Although Mr. Browning's anger found an outlet in these activities, it was all for naught. His wife, Patricia, at a loss and bereft of personal support from her crusading husband, began to drink heavily, an onerous sign of deterioration that her husband scornfully dismissed as "weakness." Neither was able to help Ethan, and for all Mr. Browning's aggressive tactics, he did not succeed in wresting his son from the Hare Krishna.

Every family is torn by guilt and recrimination. Dr. Holtzman accused his wife of alienating Phil further by being too harshly critical of him during their transatlantic calls, and at the same time told Ellen that if she hadn't constantly talked about Israel over the years all this wouldn't have happened. Yet he was so ashamed himself that he couldn't discuss the matter with his Yiddish-speaking parents, who had grown up in the same Orthodox Jewish milieu that seemed to him Phil's "sick" choice.

Linda Green was quite sure her own enthusiasm for therapy as a way of life had caused Jennifer's departure, and her husband more than agreed. For the first time in their marriage, this disinvolved man became aggressive and outspoken. "If you hadn't been so goddamn psychology crazy," he yelled at his wife, "Jennie would never have left home." However, one can assume that Mr. Green, having neglected to interfere with this "craziness" for years, felt guilty too. It was he who continued to pay the monthly bills to the Healing Workshop.

So did the Holtzmans pay for Phil's yeshiva studies throughout his stay, so did the Vitellis continue to send Fred money whenever he ran out during his time with the Armed Guard, and John Gould did not seek to change the provisions that allowed Jamie to use the income of his trust fund when he joined the Church of Scientology, and continued to support the house where Jamie still lived as well. These parents all paid for what they took to be their fault.

Many joiners have quite purposefully driven in the knife of guilt by the specific nature of their radical departure. Phil by entering a yeshiva, Jennifer by choosing a therapeutic commune, and Dennis by escaping the draft had all, in a way, said, "Here's the cake you asked for; now eat it." Their parents found it hard to swallow. In fact, they were furious at what had been jammed down their throats.

How quickly parents can recognize the rebellious nature of their child's act and respond with anger is best shown by the story of Ethan's three-week courtship with the Hare Krishna prior to his joining.

When he asked permission from his parents to visit the Hare Krishna temple for dinner on the day after he was first approached, they saw no reason to say no. It was proper for Ethan, at 16, to ask permission; it was reasonable for the Brownings, sophisticated and intelligent parents, to comply. Ethan had that gloss of maturity that the only child raised among adults often has, and his parents had become accustomed to treating him with a respect bordering on aloofness. They were merely mildly interested and tolerant of this only son's curiosity. So, after a smile and a remark that the Hare Krishna was, his father was sure Ethan realized, a cult, Ethan went through the second step in his screening process with his father's blessing.

What happened during the following week was in lieu of a retreat. Ethan spent whole afternoons, evenings, and most of the following weekend at the temple. The disinterest the Brownings had already noticed in the broad range of activities their son had once enjoyed became much worse. Indeed, this studious youngster stopped studying at all. Mrs. Browning overheard her son turning down repeated invitations from his one close friend. Ethan cut extracurricular activities so that he could spend afternoons at the temple.

By the end of that first week, Ethan began to complain about the food his parents served. It wasn't good for them; it was impure. His mother should stop buying meat and serve vegetables and rice. Though these suggestions irked Mr. Browning in particular, he still didn't want to be seen as intolerant or unreasonable, and so he remained willing to discuss diet as though it were really a family medical concern. Ethan didn't show up for dinner most nights during the following week anyway, and tension mounted.

The night Ethan lied to his mother and father about his whereabouts to cover an overnight stay with the Hare Krishna, the Brownings put their foot down. All visits to the temple were banned. Ethan was told he would have to keep his nose to the grindstone. He was to bring his schoolwork up to date, maintain his former friendships, and resume after-school activities. Further, he was to accompany his mother and father to the Episcopal church for Sunday services.

Ethan agreed, but only to avoid confrontation. He continued to visit with the Hare Krishna on the sly, and was found out. The Brownings saw that a total ban wasn't going to work. Still intent on being reasonable, they offered to strike a bargain: They would permit Ethan to visit the temple several times a week if he would agree to spend the rest of his free time at home seeing friends or pursuing his former interests. Again, Ethan agreed, and even consented to see a psychiatrist. He kept several appointments, and reported listlessly that "the guy's nice enough." The doctor reported to the Brownings that Ethan was not a disturbed child.

In a final effort at fairness, the Brownings went themselves to meet with the Hare Krishna's local leader at the temple. Reason deserted them at last. They might as well have come upon a witches' coven led by the Devil himself, so bizarre did the goings-on strike them. This was no religion; the leader, they felt, was an impostor.

Strained negotiations immediately exploded into angry confrontations. Requests became demands, pleas became commands. Voices were raised, accusations leveled, insults hurled. Finally, the desperate parents issued on ultimatum: our way or out. Ethan left.

Exactly this same story of tolerance escalating to worry, alarm, strained reasoning, futile bargains, and exploding fury could be told of many, substituting a precocious sexual affair, say, or drug experimentation for Ethan's move toward the Hare Krishna. Such scenes are repeated in hundreds of thousands of homes where adolescents act out their rebellion in ways designed to push parents hard against the wall.

The difference is that radical departers are, to the best of their awareness, not doing anything wrong. The members of Ethan's temple were not, for instance, a "bad crowd." Membership in any of these groups is chosen from just the same social background as that of the would-be joiner. This fact the new joiners recognize at once, and although their families are affronted by saffron robes and gong-playing— Mr. Browning called members "freaks"—joiners are delighted to find themselves among exactly their own kind. These adolescents simply don't join genuine Buddhist or Hindu groups, for example, or any that are truly alien to the way they were brought up.

Just as the ordinariness of the membership is only superficially costumed to seem alien to outsiders, so the values to which the group subscribes are only thinly veiled versions of middle-class ideals—all that hard work, sharing, caring, scrubbed floors, and good food. Joiners' parents could readily subscribe to such time-honored ideals if they were packaged differently.

It is no accident that the packaging of peculiar costuming and bizarre rituals is what enrages parents the most. That is exactly what the members, unbeknownst to themselves, intend. These groups offer the perfect smoke screen for children who must rebel but mustn't know that they are doing so. To parents looking only at the smoke, it seems their children have abandoned with a vengeance the kinds of people and kinds of values they had been brought up to respect. This is a slap in the face, transparent contempt for what their families stand for, and parents react with the sad sense of loss and enraged sense of betrayal parents feel at other violent forms of rebellion.

Behind the smoke, so to speak, the rebellers themselves, massed among their own kind and exalted by familiar values, are genuinely astonished at their parents' anger. They don't know they have rebelled. They are, at last, living up to the expectations they believe their parents have had of them all the time. Their "innocence," of course, makes the parody all the crueler from the family's point of view. To understand, then, the full evolution of parents' response to a radical departure, it must be kept in mind that the families are reacting quite normally.

Like Mr. Browning, the other parents of these nine joiners tried at first to be reasonable. As thoughtful and knowledgeable people, they were well aware of the existential dilemmas of adolescence and young adulthood. They recalled similar feelings they had had at that age, but the playacting quality of these groups' dress and melodramatic rituals made them view their children as having gone on an irresponsible lark. "These kids don't know what suffering is," Lillian Lewis told me, referring to the poverty of her own childhood. "I had it a lot tougher and I considered running away too. But that's a cop-out." Dr. Holtzman remarked, "Life isn't easy for anyone, not just our kids. Who doesn't want to pack it in every now and then?" And Jack Ericson finished that thought by saying, "But who can leave? Family, job, responsibilities, networks of people make it impossible. Unless, of course, you're irresponsible."

Fathers become especially prickly on the subject of responsibility. "When I was that age," complained George Lewis, "I had to think of food on the table; school was my luxury. I couldn't fart around in some crazy group. My father would have killed me."

"Self-indulgent brats" is what Stuart Browning called joiners. "If they're dissatisfied with the world, and who the hell isn't, why don't they do something positive about it instead of navel gazing and bullshit?"

While parents rail at their children's irresponsibility, joiners feel that they are at last being responsible, and in just the way their parents had wished. The Goulds, especially Joanna, were active in the Ethical Culture Society and had spearheaded various social causes. "My parents were in antinuke demonstrations before that was fashionable," Jamie mused. "They were rich, but they were always concerned about injustice and war. I know they would love Scientology. I'm surprised by their anger; I thought they'd like the idea of their son being in a group concerned about important issues."

Jennifer said of her group, "I really believe that we've achieved a new level of interaction here. I've explained to my mother how meaningful it really is. I bet that she'd join if she had a chance." That was one month into Jennifer's stay at the Healing Workshop and at the height of Mrs. Green's frantic research on how to get her out.

Nancy was incredulous that her parents were still dissatisfied with her. In keeping with their Methodist standards of behavior, she had given up her theatrical pretensions, casual sex, and drugs—all sources of previous family discussion. "Man, I used to be lazy!" she remarked of her former self, but getting up at 4:00 A.M. and working hard all day didn't impress her parents either. She had thought their concern always was for her happiness, for which they had made such sacrifices; she was happy now—would nothing ever please them?

Of all the hundreds of joiners' families I've spoken with, none were pleased with their son's or daughter's choice. The closest any family came to tolerating a radical departure during its first months was the Vitellis' response to their troublesome son Fred.

From his first call home from Rome after the Armed Guard's retreat in rural northern Italy, Fred sounded changed—but for the better. His foul tongue had been washed with a soap Maria Vitelli had never had access to; the obscenities were not gone, but they were noticeably fewer and milder. His tune of purpose and involvement struck notes his family had never heard from him before, and that encouraged them. Fred did not yet realize, nor would he have been likely to confide it anyway, how dangerous and violent this group's plans were to become, so the Vitellis at first pictured nothing more onerous than a level of protest not unusual at their son's age. They were cautiously optimistic.

Joiners don't, however, leave well enough alone. Fred soon began to preach civil disobedience, social disruption, and the virtues of anarchy to his startled and increasingly alarmed parents. Nancy felt that the only way to make peace with her family was to help them "see the light." To that end, she lectured them mercilessly on their failings when she wasn't ranting in the peculiarly irritating way of the zealot. The Lewises leaped to the bait to defend their own way of life and to attack hers. Nancy's smugness was unendurable; only a Child of God, she said, could possibly be good, selfless, and truly concerned for the welfare of others. About three months after Nancy's departure, Lillian Lewis's father became terminally ill with leukemia. He asked to see Nancy one last time before he died. Nancy, supposedly selflessly devoted to the needs of others, sent him a perfunctory note that said she was too busy to visit.

Friends are treated no more kindly than family. Phil had had particularly longstanding friendships among a group of children who had grown up together in Denver. Ordinarily, such friendships are among the most precious and enduring, but Phil made no effort to ease his friends' sense of hurt and betrayal. When two boyhood pals used their own savings to go to Jerusalem to try to talk him out of the yeshiva, he tried to convert them to his fundamentalist point of view.

Any attempt to lure a child home through reason, pleading, or argument is met at this point with a thick insolence. "What's in it for me?" Ethan threw back when asked why he would not consider returning to his family and his former life. Nancy at last agreed to a meeting with the Lewises, who traveled down to Fort Lauderdale from their home in New Jersey. "You mean you want me to give up all this to be as happy as *you*?" she scornfully replied to their pleas. No matter how unconvincing their happy faces look to those on the outside, joiners insist on being taken at face value. More, they want their families to become just like them.

Phil was by no means content to court mere tolerance. At first, he showed only that "holier than thou" smugness typical of committed members, but he would not shut up. He spewed ideology that, understandably, his father thought arguable. The two had often debated various points of view in their tradition of intellectual inquiry, and it seemed to Dr. Holtzman that abstractions were automatically within the realm of reason. Probed and questioned, however, Phil felt demeaned and ridiculed, as though his father were attempting to invalidate his aspirations. The same was true if his mother tried to get beneath his ideological armor to suggest that it might have psychological underpinnings. As with all members during their intense commitment, nothing would do but that his parents agree with him completely and experience his happiness as their own.

Or so he claimed. Actually, Phil turned to attack. He accused the Holtzmans of ignorance of their religion. He began to criticize their "heathen" diet as Reform Jews—the Holtzmans did not conform to kosher regulations—and referred to the "sinful" way his mother dressed. He exhorted them to move to Jerusalem, where they too could be "saved."

Telephone calls became shouting matches; they invariably ended with Sam Holtzman and Phil mutually enraged, and Ellen in tears.

This time of escalating anger is immune to humor. One can't rib a radical departer. One can't even make a joke of one's own failings. Joiners smile, sometimes radiantly, but they don't laugh. Every family knows the relief when some former disaster—that may really have been quite painful—is transformed into a family joke, and many potential thrusts from a rebelling teenager are parried by teasing. There is no teasing even among the members themselves, as though there were some unspoken pact never to let loose the guffaw that might bring down each other's house of cards.

Without humorous perspective, and certainly without the benevolence joiners affect, pummeling with insults and criticism continues until parents feel bruised and beaten. Ethan's father planned one last, desperate attack: a kidnapping. "If we hadn't done that, we would never have forgiven ourselves," he explained. "We felt we were losing him." And, when the plan failed, he said, "I felt as if I had been in a long battle, and that I had lost. We were wiped out, drained physically and emotionally."

Nancy's family retired from the battlefield. An icy silence grew between her and her parents; they discontinued all communication for several months. "For a while," Mrs. Lewis recalled, "we felt Nancy was no longer part of us. I remember crying constantly and acting as if she were dead."

There is a kind of mourning at this point, and although the child isn't really "lost" or "dead," there is a psychological basis for mourning. The child in which these parents had invested so much of themselves and in whose self they had in turn participated has become distant and alien. The Suzanne of the bubbly laughter had vanished. Slender Ethan, windblown and salt-sprayed as he raced his boat, was gone. To these parents, their child's future, which should have been theirs to enjoy, is gone too. No daughter starring in the ice show, no son following his father's footsteps into engineering, and, as far as they can see, no homecomings, no graduations, no celebrations they could ever share again. The part of themselves that was that child seems to them lost or dead.

So they let their child go, or try to.

"After a while," Dr. Holtzman explained, "you give up ranting and raving. Life has to go on. We had our careers, our other three children. Phil wasn't going to be changed back again by our anger and our tears. Inside, we were in despair, but we tried to bury it and go on with living. We stopped bugging him about his mistake."

By this stage, six months at least, and perhaps a year or more, have passed. Parents turn to the last portion of the task radical departures demand of them: to rebuild their own sense of self at a distance from their child, and from this distance to find some basis for a rapprochement with him.

Charles and Kate O'Connor sought rapprochement. "We just decided that Kathy felt it was her duty to convert others to the Divine Light Mission. We obviously weren't going to be swayed, and we had let her know we wanted her to stop moralizing to us. She stopped, although we were still aware of how she wanted us to run our lives. We found other things to talk about."

Perhaps Jack Ericson put parents' need for rapprochement most movingly. "We knew after a while that we couldn't convince Dennis to walk away from 3HO. And he knew that we could never bring ourselves to like what he had done. But he was still our son, we loved him dearly, and we didn't want to lose that."

Children respond to the moratorium with a de-escalation of their own. When the Lewises were able to write to Nancy again, she was able to write to them. Suzanne affected an air of tolerance—her parents were more to be pitied now than insulted or accused. Dennis still thought his family close-minded, but could "agree to disagree."

The strength of rapprochement depends, however, on what has preceded it. One would have to include the entire period of the O'Connors' bitter disappointment in Kathy from the time of her affair with Michael in counting up how long it took them to attempt rapprochement. That time came to a total of nearly four years—too long to patch up easily the differences between them. In general, the longer the battle, the more fragile the peace treaty.

Also, the bitterer the war has been, the less trust the child will feel when offers of peace are tendered. Phil's shouting matches with the Holtzmans had risen to such a pitch of animosity that in spite of their decision not to "bug him"—an understatement if there ever was one—his anger remained at the ready. No one easily forgets the bare face of fury.

Complete schism doesn't augur well for a reliable rapprochement either. When Nancy's parents stopped writing or calling her for months, she felt they had broken their bonds with her altogether, and even they claimed she was "dead" to them. Doing actual harm to a child, as Stuart Browning did by the shocking betrayal of kidnapping, cuts through the last strands of trust a child may harbor.

Genuine rapprochement isn't possible until parents are able, like the Ericsons, to love their child *as he is now*, rather than as they used to love him. Sam and Ellen Holtzman, down deep where their "burying" had been done, clung to a Phil who was unchanged. A much stronger basis for rebuilding a relationship occurs when new perspectives allow both generations to find good in the other regardless of the failings they also perceive.

All of this is of more than academic interest, for the strength of rapprochement between parents and their son or daughter and the time it takes to get there have a profound effect on the child's psychological reorganization during the period of his departure. The sooner rapprochement comes, and the stronger it is, the earlier the child's return to home and family.

The work is hard because, not only are parents forced to compress their own reorganization into months instead of the years usually allowed by other children's gradual separation, but also the sustaining rewards most children offer in the form of laudable accomplishments are absent. Parents are deprived of mutuality; they must work on their own to separate from their child unilaterally.

The Greens were able to come to a rapprochement with Jennifer about eight months into her stay at the Healing Workshop. Linda Green's exhaustive but uninformative research had by then pulled her only rug of defense from under her. One weekend there was another fight with her husband on Saturday; his criticisms continued during Sunday. That evening, she dissolved in unwonted tears.

Allen Green assumed control. With an accountant's pragmatism, he reasoned out their predicament to his suddenly helpless wife. Intellectualizing had not resolved either personal or family difficulties, he said. The bottom line was the reality of their attachment to one another. He had never shared his wife's enthusiasms; he had always thought her wrong. But disagreement need not lead to desertion. Here he was, still steadfast in his love for her. He felt the same about Jennifer. They had to tell her so.

Jason, home for a weekend from graduate school, joined his father in this firm stand, and Mrs. Green "came to," as she put it to me the following month. Jason agreed to act as intermediary, and by the time I interviewed the family they had made clear to Jennifer that despite their fear and disapproval, they stood ready to help in whatever ways a family can help when and if she needed them. Jennifer herself "came to" eight weeks later. Of these nine joiners, her radical departure of eleven months was the shortest.

The course of a radical departure is ultimately controlled by the joiner's own internal development. One can't get inside a child's mind and rearrange his perceptions for him. Parents can, however, change what there is for him to perceive: his actual relationship with his family.

If parents can avoid panicking at the first news of a radical departure, they may be able to change their relationship with their child at the outset. The Holtzmans might have admitted to being astonished at Phil's decision, worried by it, and also opposed to it. They could have added that, since he was 21, they declined to tell him how to run his life. Of course, they could have said, they also need not pay for decisions they thought unwise, and if he wished to stay in the yeshiva, he would have to pay for it himself.

Such a tactic, when it is emotionally possible for parents, unilaterally withdraws them from the dependent relationship their child has with them. At the same time, it diminishes in his perception the destructive power he imagines he has over his parents. He can aim to hurt but—and this will be a relief to the joiner—they are reliably strong.

During the first days and even weeks after joining, new members are still in a somewhat confused state of mind. They may not return simply because parents have left the door open, but if parents can keep their own perspective, intense commitment may be avoided, and the child's stay may be a transient one. Unfortunately, however, emotional reactions tend to become so intense so quickly that timely detachment is not possible.

Since, for the purposes of my studies, I interviewed only fully committed members who had been within the group for at least six months, what I saw were almost invariably families, parents and children alike, who had reacted very emotionally to one another. As described, detachment occurred only after parents had gone through an intense period of protest, followed by mourning. The amount of time required for a family to complete the process and arrive at rapprochement with their child varied a great deal. That is, I think, where to look for a way to help a radical departer toward his or her return.

Faced with what seems to them at the time a tragic loss, parents need the same sort of support they seek during other personal crises. Emotions subside as they are shared with others. Perspective is gained as others contribute their points of view. Renewed interest in one's own life is renewed by others' insistence. Rapprochement is eased through the participation of outside parties.

Individual therapists and group support systems have both speeded along parents' own separation from their child in many cases I have seen. The Lewises were helped to resign themselves to the actuality of Nancy's leave-taking, to mourn her loss, and then to reorganize their sense of who they were and what they stood for by a psychiatrist. They consulted her in their own behalf only as a last resort; their original idea had been to seek a way to get their daughter back, not to resign themselves to her absence. I think consultation in one's own behalf should be the first resort. The less time spent in futile protest, the better.

One need not seek a therapist with special expertise in radical departures. The psychological reorganization the departure occasions is similar to that necessitated by other crises in a family's life, and therapists in general are familiar with it. I would suggest that both parents participate in the therapy, and it may be that other children in the family are upset enough by the disruption of their accustomed lives that they will need support as well. Seeing a therapist as a family will also quickly dispel notions of blame, which only stand in the way of everyone's recovery.

Self-help groups are less expensive and are probably as helpful a way of getting through the hard work of recovery. By self-help group, I don't mean vigilantes who are themselves mired in futile and obsessive protest. There are, instead, groups of parents who are suffering or have suffered radical departures and who simply wish to share the pain. They have the advantage that they are in various stages of their recovery, and their children are in various stages of their departure or return, and so they can offer a balance of sympathy and perspective. Ministers and rabbis, mental health associations, and "hot lines" listed in the telephone directory yellow pages are all sources for locating such groups.

As parents begin to feel the intensity of their emotion subsiding and their interest in other matters returning, they can actually make practical plans for rapprochement. The Greens were able to engage their grown son's services as a go-between to Jennifer, and I have often seen similarly neutral, trusted relatives or friends perform this role well.

Other sorts of emotionally neutral communication are also possible. Mrs. Marquette's frequent letters simply stating what the rest of the family was doing—buying a new car, extending the vegetable garden, taking a vacation together—were a good choice. The facts will stand by themselves: as individuals, mothers and fathers have other interests besides their child and his plans to save the world.

If the family has been resentfully paying for a child's upkeep or making donations to his cause, such support payments should be withdrawn. The withdrawal should not be done with rancor. There are ways to spend money that seem more worthwhile, and although it is clear the child doesn't see it that way, it is not his decision to make.

Most communication with the joiner may have been by telephone or visit. During these, parents can make it clear that they will not be shouted at, harangued, or preached to. They like the kind of people they are and the way they conduct their life; they intend to continue as they have been. As parents, they will listen respectfully to their child's perspectives and they expect to be listened to with similar respect.

One shouldn't expect much effect from all this at first. Mrs. Marquette's letters frequently went unanswered, and Phil continued to shout. By being true to themselves, however, mothers and fathers make clear that they have, albeit unilaterally, now achieved the distance their child is himself still seeking.

Distance and integrity are one side of rapprochement. The other side is love. It may be that emotion has nearly sundered the family relationship during the torments of protest and mourning—to a frozen silence, as with the Lewises, or terrible animosity, as with the Holtzmans. It is important now for parents to admit that things have gone too far, but that the height of their response no longer expresses their true feelings. Children need to hear that parents will be there when they are needed. With that out of the way, the Lewises were able cheerfully to invite Nancy to visit them for a Fourth of July picnic, the Greens chose a modest personal gift for Jennifer's birthday, and the Ericsons could sympathize with Dennis when he wasn't feeling well. Prior to rapprochement, families are all too liable to use family occasions as wellsprings of incrimination and to snidely withhold gifts and sympathy from joiners who claim they have no material or spiritual needs beyond what their group supplies. Families should by all means visit when time and finances allow, and should try not to let any long periods of time to elapse between communication of one sort or another. Sooner or later, the unilateral nature of parents' rapprochement is met with reciprocity.

So far, these joiners have seemed to be shut down, on vacation from growing up, so to speak. But as parents complete their end of the separation, they make the relationship itself safer for their children. In this fertile ground are planted the first visible seeds of progress: doubts and longings that now begin to assail these previously impenetrable zealots.

6

Seeds of Doubt

After a period of some months to a year or more within the group, there begins to be a subtle but unmistakable change in the joiner. Within the fabric of uniform perceptions, intense commitment, and total entrenchment, gaps develop. Dogmatic attitudes relax somewhat; there are fewer unequivocal opinions and there is less inflexible faith. The change usually begins after the first year of membership, but it can occur two years or more later and occasionally well before the first year is over.

Timing isn't exactly in accord with parents' attempts at rapprochement, but is usually in some rhythm with it. Some softening in Philip Holtzman's zeal seemed to come as a response to his father's decision to stop dwelling on his son's "mistake," whereas the Vitellis seemed ready to renegotiate their relationship with Fred as a response to his own dwindling interest in protest. Where the schism has been least bitter and complete—frequently due to the mother's abiding compassion—the ground may be prepared within months after departure but may still await a definitive event to trigger the change. On the other hand, potential triggers may fail if there seems to be no one in the outside world willing to receive the changed member of a radical group.

Whenever the relaxation begins, it is quickly followed by a siege of doubting the perfection of the group and its leader, an upwelling of longing for the family, and finally a return to the outside world.

Some joiners are able to identify the specific event that seemed to trigger their doubts, or that crystallized doubts that up until that point had been vague and not much charged with emotion. Others can't recall any such experience but do describe a gradual ambiguity creeping into a faith that had only shortly before been certain and absolute.

The trigger that set off Fred's decision to return home eighteen months after his departure was a literal one; a member of the Armed Guard had two fingers blown off while setting the firing mechanism of a small bomb. Fred announced his departure right then and there, but for some time he had been experiencing doubt amid a wave of increasing lonesomeness for his family.

Members of the Armed Guard were not surprised. They knew perfectly well that Fred had joined initially more out of attraction to Yvette than through ideological conviction. That love affair had in fact been short-lived, and a bout of promiscuity afterward only helped to cement the group's opinion of him as a "lightweight." Although he was involved with endless plans—to put forth radical candidates; to demonstrate against the visit of a U.S. warship, an ambassador, the carrying out of a policy; to bomb a military installation—he was not encouraged to take an active part in strategy and certainly was not given any role in acts of vandalism. "I suppose they thought I'd fuck up," Fred finally realized.

Gradually, political discussion and continual intrigue began to seem tedious and ineffective. A comparison arose in his mind. His suspicion that the Armed Guard might not be so admirable a group of people as he had thought was very like his previous scorn for friends and family. Perhaps his burden of contempt was his own problem, and not a reflection of the outside world. With this thought, there emerged crushing regret for how shabbily he had treated his parents and a longing to see them again.

The Vitellis caught this more engaging tone during telephone conversations with him, and with some longing themselves recalled for him family times that had been dear to all of them. The last remnants of Fred's unattractive façade began to crumble. He no longer felt he could beat the system, in either his father's business domain or the political world; he wanted to go to college. The frightening bomb accident galvanized his growing desire to go home and pursue his new plan.

Incredibly, it was only then that it occurred to him that the group he had been committed to for a year and a half were terrorists; he had thought of the Armed Guard only as political activists, although his father had used the word "terrorist" often enough during the preceding year.

Criticism from a member's family or from society at large rarely is heard until it is "reheard" during the period of doubt. Kathy O'Connor, for example, had been deaf and blind to both her family's and the media's insistence on the Maharaj Ji's shabby character for three full years of devotion in his Divine Light Mission. But dissension within the group can have a devastating effect, as it did on her, and then the message quite suddenly comes in loud and clear.

To Kathy, a most distasteful aspect of her life within her family had been the emphasis on creature comforts and on display of material worth. The field of nursing appealed to her precisely because, in her view, a nurse's individualism is subjugated to the care of others; worth is measured by altruism. Indeed, the nurse's uniform reassured her that others could not judge her personal value by crass external trappings. When she joined the Divine Light Mission, their simplicity appealed to her utterly. She gratefully submerged herself in asceticism, love, and devotion to her Perfect Master.

The O'Connors tried to tell Kathy what they had heard about this Perfect Master. He had rows of yachts displayed on the grounds of his mansion. The money so painstakingly collected by his followers was spent, not on saving the world, but on shocking self-aggrandizement and a vulgar show of luxury. "Liars!" she had yelled in reply. "Sinners!"

Her "beautiful master," she knew, did live better than his followers. The group explained why this was so: "If you're going to deal with the Devil and beat him you have to seduce him first." This made perfect sense to Kathy at the time. Her parents stopped arguing about it.

Kathy had been in the Divine Light Mission for three years when she attended a rally that, for the first time, caused her to feel the shock of doubt. There must have been 20,000 people there, awaiting the arrival of the Maharaj Ji. For several hours the audience was prepared for his entry by professional music and dance performances and by the moving experience of so many thousands of voices joined in prayer. The Perfect Master arrived. He sat on a white leather throne surrounded by banks of flowers and surmounted by gold banners, and he was served by a host of high priests. The focal point of the stage was a huge papier-mâché model of a diamond.

Kathy was momentarily aghast. The display was vulgar. The man wallowed in luxury. More money had gone into the performance, the staging, and the stage set than had been spent on any performance she had ever attended. Where was simplicity here?

For several days words of doubt (the Divine Light Mission is a fraud) and disillusioning images (the Maharaj Ji lolling on a yacht) pushed their way into her mind. But she persevered in her attempts to believe in her Perfect Master. After all, for years now she had steadfastly put public criticism and her parents' "rumormongering" down to jealousy, ignorance, and prejudice.

That year, however, was 1976, and the Maharaj Ji was about to be deposed in favor of his brother. That act was a final horror to Kathy. How does one dump a "perfect" spiritual leader? When the Maharaj Ji's own mother and brother joined the chorus of criticism against her master, she could only conclude that the accusations were valid. Her finest feelings betrayed, she left the group.

Jamie Gould also began to doubt the perfection of Scientology during a period of dissension within the church, but, although the resulting disillusion did trigger his leaving the group, he didn't suffer Kathy's sense of emotional devastation or of personal betrayal. The group was undergoing major changes in 1980. L. Ron Hubbard, its founder and messianic leader, was at that time thought by its members to be dead. (A California District Court three years later, in June 1983, ruled that Hubbard "must be" alive.) The church was assailed by countless lawsuits, not the least of which was one initiated by Hubbard's son, and it had been charged with tax evasion in a number of jurisdictions. Police raids, media exposés, and accusations of misdemeanors and malfeasance were rampant all over the world; the church seemed to be in a state of siege.

At first, this atmosphere of universal condemnation served to strengthen the resolve of Jamie and his confreres. There was a feeling of "us against the world," a curious sense of security in being persecuted. But when criticism began coming from even the inner sanctum of Hubbard's family and closest advisers, Jamie, his girlfriend Julia, and some of their best friends in the group felt a pall of doubt.

They were too ashamed of their changed perceptions to share them immediately with one another, but by this time Jamie had been living with Julia for a year and soon dared to confide his growing disillusion to her. Julia in turn was relieved to hear her own doubts echoed. Fortified by one another, they gradually opened up to their most intimate friends, and in the process discovered that an unusual number of members were contemplating leaving. Over the next weeks, discussions became more avid and quite practical. Plans were made of whom to inform, what jobs they might seek, and where they might go. While a mass defection did not take place, about a dozen members, some of whom had been highly respected "clears," left the Church of Scientology in unison. Jamie and Julia were among them.

Parents and society at large realize how vulnerable members of these groups are to discovering the imperfections—if not the perfidies—of their leaders. Certainly one focus of their efforts to disentangle young people from their odd devotion has been to unmask unseemly behavior, hypocrisy, and even criminality in particularly charismatic leaders of cultlike groups. The effort does sometimes pay off, when the real shoddiness of a group leader is publicly exposed. But in my experience members themselves are taken in only during their period of commitment, and with or without comment from the outside world they themselves come to perceive the truth when their own development allows them to bear it. Until that time, virtually no amount of arguing, correcting, or confrontation with the facts will be convincing. More likely, in the period of commitment, criticism will only corroborate

the members' view of the critics as malevolent, ignorant, and igno-
minious. When the seeds of doubt are ready to be planted, outside
cajoling may be seen as supportive but by then it is also unnecessary;
the switch back is internally thrown. Jennifer Green's mother, for example, never was able to find out much about Kurt, the suave "father"
of the Healing Workshop, and the group had never achieved the sort
of notoriety that attracts the scandal-hungry media. Nevertheless, Jennifer came to see Kurt as the philanderer he was.

By the time the fabric of Jennifer's commitment began to come
apart, after nearly a year of membership in the Healing Workshop, she
had become a senior member, with the responsibility for soon opening
a new branch, on the West Coast. She was to be its director. Though
this might have been the high point of her devotion, quite the opposite was true. She had become aware that Kurt, the group founder,
leader, and also her lover, slept with other women as well. She denied
jealousy to herself and to others, and even after she left the group she
maintained to me that she had no sense that her love for Kurt had
been either unrequited or betrayed. Yet, as she said, she suddenly "woke
up." "It sounds ridiculous, I know," she confided, "but after being in
the Healing Workshop for eleven months I suddenly got this sense that
this was all bullshit. It was as if I had suddenly woken up from a vivid
dream; not a bad dream, but still very real, very dramatic. And I couldn't
believe the things I was saying, let alone anyone else in the Workshop."

In this new light, Jennifer saw easily why her parents had been upset: she had given up the piano for a seriously flawed dream. Kurt now
appeared blemished—a hypocrite who, while professing simplicity and
selflessness, was actually self-indulgent and uncaring. "From a god to
an asshole," she said to me, incredulously and self-mockingly. Looking around at herself and her fellow members, she couldn't find a trace
of the self-realization that had been all she had talked about for so many
months. She was soon ready to return home.

Many former members can't put their finger on the one realization
or the single event that marked the beginning of their doubts. Even
when they can, such moments mark only their realization of doubt
and not the loosening of bonds with the group that are noticeable to

others. The transition from blissful belonging during the height of their commitment, to a straddling of the boundary between group and home during rapprochement, to a doubting so strong that a return to the outside world is inevitable can take months and creep up so gradually that the person is not aware of it. Nancy Lewis showed signs of wear in her enthusiasm that were noticeable to her peers within the group well before they reached her own awareness.

During most of her eighteen months as a member of the Children of God, she dismissed her parents with the withering label "poor misguided souls." She threw herself with great energy into the many activities that seemed to her enlightened in contrast to the way outsiders lived. But gradually her companions began to notice a slackening of her interest. She joined communal singing and praying less often, and was less fervent when she did attend. The Passion plays that had initially been a purified replacement for the "life upon the wicked stage" of her previous fantasy no longer absorbed her. Most noticeable to fellow members, her "return"—the money she received through her "litnessing" efforts to sell Children of God literature and to proselytize—was way down. When questioned by her group about her withdrawal of interest, Nancy denied it vehemently and genuinely. She was hurt that they could entertain so malicious a criticism. Yet she began to write letters home as the ice between her and her family thawed somewhat. Their tone was only tentatively warm at first, as if she were testing the waters.

But still Nancy remained in the group, and even volunteered to resettle yet again in this nomadic belonging, this time in a new communal home in Philadelphia. It was just after she had resettled there that she made a move that she herself did not recognize as significant. She consented to a visit from her cousin Becky and Becky's fiancé, Robert. She remembered feeling that she would be safe with Becky, as she had always been. Becky had been critical of her when she had left originally, but more with concern than hostility. There was no threat that she'd be taken away; she could trust this cousin.

Sitting in a coffee shop with the engaged couple, Nancy thought how much in love they looked. Becky was bringing her up to date on what she had been doing lately. She was finishing her occupational-therapy degree; Robert was in law school at Rutgers. They had plans for careers, marriage—the future.

Nancy suddenly was seized with self-doubt. What have I been doing with myself? she recalled thinking. The future loomed before her, and something had, as she put it so clearly, "unsnapped." Every remnant of her fervor evaporated during a mere two hours of the most ordinary conversation. She went back to the group that afternoon to propose a visit to New Jersey to see her parents.

What impresses me the most about the growth of these doubts in the young men and women is how unbidden it is. The person doesn't consciously assess his or her situation, compare it to alternatives, decide to listen to others' perceptions, or even determine to repair what, somewhere down deep, they must know to be the damage they have wrought. Instead, words well up, images appear, emotions overtake them—and they are as incapable of resisting them as they are innocent of summoning them. Suzanne Marquette's experience is particularly evocative of this strange process by which thoughts and feelings simply rise to the surface of what had seemed for months to be an impenetrable thickness of defense.

For nearly two years Suzanne had merely "regretted"—this was the strongest word she was willing to use—the telephone altercations between her father and herself. That trace of regret did little to moderate her conviction that breaking away from her family had been for the best. During the last few months of her commitment, she felt some relief, since her mother had managed to put an end to her father's long onslaught, although she thought her relief was due to the fact that she could concentrate exclusively on making her life with the Moonies as meaningful as possible. When I spoke with her at this point, she honestly didn't feel upset about having deserted her family, nor did she have the slightest sense of missing her old life.

When thoughts of her family did begin to intrude, they were in the form of wondering how they were and what they were doing, but these musings were not accompanied by any deep feeling. She was still devoted to the Reverend Sun Myung Moon and all he stood for, but the fervor had lessened, and her convictions were less tenacious. It was in this "relaxed" frame of mind that her emotions surfaced in a star-

tling and upsetting fashion. She remembered sitting in the warm sun
with Moonie friends. All was peaceful and calm, as it had been at her
first meeting with the group, on the day of her audition. Yet she suddenly started crying. The only thing that she could think of at the time
was: I wish I was with Mom and Dad. Her friends comforted her,
thinking she was tired.

The unreasonable bout of tears and the homesick words that accompanied it upset Suzanne, and she didn't talk about the episode.
Over the next few days this thought and others like it continued to
appear unbidden in her consciousness. Try as she might to get rid of
them, the longings became even stronger. Her mind was filled with
recollections of her childhood, her blond brothers—in first grade now—
and the work she had done as a volunteer in the retirement home. She
saw a poster advertising "Holiday on Ice" at the Cow Palace in San
Francisco, and she was overwhelmed with sadness.

"I began thinking about skating again. I surprised myself, because
I thought that I was clear that I never wanted to skate again."

All of a sudden—"maybe three weeks, although it felt like hours"—
Suzanne knew that she wanted to leave, to go back home again.

In many ways the period during which joiners nourish seeds of doubt
echoes the period of self-doubt prior to their radical departure. The
leader of the group, once perceived to be as perfect as a child supposes
his parents are, is revealed to be flawed, a god with feet of clay. Beliefs
once accepted with childlike faith and with a child's lack of comprehension begin to seem less significant, sometimes hypocritical, even
nonsensical. The formerly committed member now entertains rebellious thoughts and contemplates breaking away. But there is a difference: this time he *knows* what he is doing and *feels* the conflict of his
impending separation.

Phil, for example, found himself increasingly irritated with the head
rabbi, who persisted in lecturing him on theological issues just as he
began to long for home; yet he had felt no anger at his parents at the
time of leaving them to join the yeshiva. Kathy's doubts about the Maharaj Ji struck her as shockingly rebellious, though she hadn't been
aware of rebellious feelings when she joined. Suzanne cried with
homesickness, and also wept to think of leaving the Moonies, her home

and family for well over a year. She hadn't suffered ambivalence upon breaking away from her real family. Jamie expected members of his group to be angry with him for wishing to leave; when he joined he had expected his parents to be delighted.

All these feelings are ones that most children experience as they make their painful withdrawal from their earlier bonds with parents. They are disappointed with their mothers and fathers, angry in return; they wish to leave, but long to stay. Yet at the time of their joining, radical departers appear to be conflict-free. They don't immediately sense their own rebelliousness, don't anticipate an angry response from parents, and don't miss them even when the schism appears to be complete. What has happened that the same person who could break away from family ties without knowing he had done so or feeling the repercussions can now reenact his original rebellion knowingly and with the full panoply of appropriate emotion?

I'm convinced that a radical departure is a rehearsal for separation, a "let's pretend" practice for the real-life task of growing up. Although members appear to be passively frozen into the narrow mold of commitment, they are actively preparing for their coming out.

The dramatic play of younger children is comparable. All through childhood boys and girls seek safe playing grounds on which to try out various life skills that they are by no means ready to attempt for real. By playing house, school, store, and myriad other enactments tailored to individual needs, children test their comprehension of how the adult world works and how they might function within it. Like the activities of radical groups, these rehearsals are often stereotyped, ritualized, and repetitious. But in the process, children in both age groups gain actual skills.

Committed members, of course, play house, school, and store on a grand scale. More significant, the game is played at a level much closer to the real world. There is no play money here, but real dollars and cents. The lessons joiners memorize are intended to be applicable in the world at large and are attempts to grapple with mankind's most pressing issues. The stove, food, and house are real too, and there is genuine basis for pride as these young men and women find that they really can support and care for themselves without the help of their parents. By the time members are ready to come out of rehearsal, they trust the actuality of their performance in ways that they did not when they first joined their troupe.

Young children also use dramatic play to gain control over impulses and emotions that might otherwise overwhelm their as yet minimal internal controls. They let a puppet lion wreak havoc and then, switching voices, scold or soothe the lion back to civilized behavior. When practice convinces them that they can control anger and negotiate conflict at a safe distance from themselves, they put puppets aside and conduct feelings and negotiations internally.

This too is comparable to the group enactment of a radical departure. But, again, the play verges closely on reality. The biting hostility of the Children of God and the social mayhem of the Armed Guard are much more dangerous than the carryings-on of a puppet beast. Yet the benevolent actors themselves feel as safe as children, and parents and society, although they are disrupted, are not destroyed. Conflict conducted externally—the good groups versus the bad world—begins to feel less threatening; it is "ineffective," Fred Vitelli realized at the same time that he came to think of his burden of contempt as a personal problem. The new perceptions that invade members during their period of doubt mark the reentry into their conscious minds of unwanted feelings that were cast out and disavowed during all the time of commitment. That members can now allow the battle to move indoors, so to speak, indicates that the structure to contain conflict has been fortified.

That structure is the selfhood that was so fragile before the radical departure, and that in its now strengthened form is also derived from the safe playing ground of group membership. Members use the unreal "model family" in which they participate as though it were real. While appearing to relinquish a private life, each exploits the model for private purposes. Group skills become individual skills and are the joiner's to enjoy as a person in his own right. Group regulation and decision-making are translated into self-regulation and self-direction. The group self provides a model for separate selfhood.

This is what the child might have been able to do within his actual family if his perception of himself as separate had not proved so frightening. Paradoxically, it is the safety of union with the model family that allows him to test his separation from his actual family, and the conflict-free state of commitment that gives him the strength to deal with conflict.

The fact that joining wasn't accompanied by conflict gives away its "as if" nature. Why should the child have *felt* what he was doing? He was only pretending. Now the actors are ready to come out of rehearsal and to try the thrust to adulthood for real. They feel it very much.

The period of doubting through which members go before their return is not only hard on them, but also threatening to their group. While they are straddling the boundary between group and home and are letting goodness and badness meet inside themselves, other members still require the verisimilitude of their performance. Doubting members, like parents and therapists who probe too hard or challenge too aggressively, threaten to unmask them before they have had time properly to arrange their own true faces. Indeed, it was Nancy Lewis's unconvincing performance that first upset her fellows, and their response was to try hard to make her again play her role with necessary fervor.

When such efforts fail, the group that the departing member is now rebelling against and breaking away from sees the departure the same way the departer sees it: as a defection. The leave-taking is apt to be fraught with the same shock, recrimination, anger, fear, sadness, and guilt that is the particular stew of rebellion within a family. But the drama that is ordinarily conducted over years of family life can be, in this symbolic family, compressed into a tumultuous few days. Unlike an actual family, the group is, after all, made up of children who lack inner strength. They can't endure challenge for long; the uncooperative actor is often immediately howled off their communal stage.

The worst sort of leave-taking is exemplified by Jennifer Green, Philip Holtzman, and Nancy Lewis.

Once Jennifer recognized that her new antagonism to the empty catch phrases of the Healing Workshop made her position there untenable, she decided to reveal her criticisms to her fellow senior members. They were shocked. A few reacted with a display of sympathy, as if Jennifer were merely going through a rough personal time and needed a heavy dose of compassion, but most were openly hostile. They told her that she was selfish and that she was being destructive to the group—something that, given the group self members rely on, is never forgivable.

The senior members, excluding Jennifer, met with Kurt privately. Their decision was that she should leave the Workshop at once, but they didn't tell her this directly. Instead, they called a general meeting of the whole group, nearly 100 strong, and presented the "facts" of her change of heart. She was portrayed varyingly as a turncoat, a failure, and a psychopath, a favorite epithet in the human-potential movement. At times the meeting had the shrill hysteria of an inquisition or the cold vindictiveness of a kangaroo court—with the same predetermined outcome. There was no doubt that Jennifer was "guilty as charged"; not only could she not protest her innocence, but she was not given the opportunity to say anything. Not a single friend stood up for her during that meeting; no word of sympathy for her was expressed. She was deeply shaken. The group to whom she had belonged body and soul for nearly a year had turned its back on her in a quick about-face—although no quicker than her own.

The whole process of Jennifer's leaving or, more accurately, her expulsion from the group, took exactly twenty-six hours from the moment she expressed her feelings to the time, bags packed, sad, frightened—and relieved—she left the Healing Workshop.

Doubts can creep up more slowly and yet the leave-taking can be as violently rejecting as Jennifer's. As Phil was given increasing responsibilities within the yeshiva, he was subjected to inevitable comparisons between professions of his faith and the actualities of its practices. The head rabbi, preoccupied with fund-raising, scorned those who lived a secular life, yet curried favor with them when it was "right"—that is, when the yeshiva needed private donations or government funding. Patriotic zeal for the Jewish homeland is at the heart of Zionism, yet Phil's yeshiva supported religious exemption from the Israeli Army. These discrepancies surfaced slowly in his mind, and didn't affect his performance to a noticeable degree.

Only after some months of doubt did he express his concerns to several fellow members and the rabbi he most trusted. Perhaps he should leave, he confided, confused as he was about his faith. The group immediately mounted a campaign to show Phil the error of his ways. At first, they were persuasive and very understanding, even confiding that his doubts were akin to ones they had experienced in the past. This was, they explained, a supreme test by God, Who, in His wisdom, was measuring the worth of this promising young man by placing before him the temptations of the material world. Fearing for his spiritual safety, they pointed out the dangers of giving in to the seductiveness of sinful thoughts. They challenged him intellectually at the same time that they warmed him with hugs and told him of their sorrow to think he could even consider abandoning them.

Phil was touched; he could follow their arguments and sympathize with their feelings. But the doubt remained, and he wanted to go home.

When it became apparent to the group that he was not being swayed, a meeting with the head rabbi was arranged. He was an impressive man whose combination of brilliance and reserve kept his students in awe. He exuded strength and wisdom, and Phil had always found him somewhat intimidating. The rabbi expressed confidence that he would stay, and that he would make a major contribution to the Jewish people. He was cerebral in his approach. "How could I tell him," Phil said to me after his return, "that I missed my girl and my friends, while he was preaching ethics and theology?"

The meeting was followed by an abrupt change in the behavior of concerned members and rabbis. Accustomed to constant company, Phil was now left alone. When he entered a room, conversation stopped and backs turned. Fellow students were "too tired" or "didn't feel like" praying with him. He was no longer asked to do special tasks or rituals. "Yours will be a wasted life," one zealous young rabbi warned him. "Here you serve God; out there is a world of sin." This primitive shunning approach backfired. Phil grew angry with the group's hostility and intolerance; his anger strengthened his resolve.

But the threats weighed on him. He was still a believer and had genuine misgivings about returning to the secular world. Although he did maintain his resolve, and did leave the yeshiva, its rejecting behavior left him fearing retribution for his faltering devotion.

When Nancy broached the subject of a visit to her parents in New Jersey, the Children of God closed ranks. She was "blissed" (perhaps an unintentional but nevertheless telling pun on "blitzed") with love, hugs, and encouragement by the entire membership. A similar procedure is called "love-bombing" by ambivalent Moonies. Nancy was constantly accompanied, and the writings of Reverend Berg, Uncle Mo, were endlessly read and interpreted to her.

She found it difficult to withstand this relentless group pressure. She soon wilted, retracted her request to visit her family, and temporarily succumbed to the barrage of bliss. Although she once again poured herself into the Children of God, her doubts returned, with even greater vehemence, after only a few days.

This time, she was much more secretive. She let no one know of the return of her doubts and questions. While out litnessing, she slipped into a phone booth to call her parents and tell them that she was contemplating returning home. The rest of the group saw her, however, surrounded the booth and hung up the receiver before the call could be completed. The blissing-blitz continued with renewed vigor.

After four more days of "benevolent" pressure, Nancy had become almost frantic to leave and decided that the only way that she could pull it off was by subterfuge. She had no money. She planned to skim what she could get by litnessing and take the first possibility of escape that arose. As it turned out, she didn't need time to amass the cash. When downtown litnessing the next day, she noticed that she was momentarily alone, and took off like a child pursued by ghosts. She ran through the crowded streets of Philadelphia, ducked in and out of department stores, zigzagged through a bus station for what seemed like an eternity, always imagining that the Children of God were right behind her. Finally, she called her parents collect. They wired her money, and she returned home on the next bus.

Such frightening, even haunted departures may fit our usual image of the need to escape from malevolent groups, but they are not typical leave-takings. When Jamie Gould left the Church of Scientology with that group of like-minded members two years after joining, their period of disillusion had been protracted, they had had time to discuss with one another how they might get along in the outside world, and they had formulated their first steps at least. Those who didn't leave at that time were angry, but anger against a dozen friends tends more to consolidate their sense of purpose than to beset them with fear. Also, Jamie "left" only figuratively; he and Julia still lived together in the New York house he had occupied since long before his departure.

Fred Vitelli left the Armed Guard with their agreement, if not with their blessing, eighteen months after his acceptance into the group. Because he had never fully participated in his group's constantly elevated anger at "the system"—and had even suggested those times out to go fishing or to picnic at the beach—his radical companions had never invested as much faith in him as he felt he had invested in them. Also, although a badge of faithfulness to the group was their mutual promise not to betray their comrades, it was a loose arrangement that meant more in the whistle-blowing department than in Fred's less alarming decision to leave. There were no recriminations or accusations. After two weeks, during which he considered his decision quite carefully, he flew home on a nonstop flight from Rome to Chicago.

The member who is leaving under a barrage of antagonism, recrimination, and threat may react with great emotional pain and fear, but the group need not be aggressive for the person who is leaving to feel wounded. Guilt and insecurity can plague the departing member even when the group is reasonable and understanding.

Much as the Moonies may be one of the more notorious of the groups these young people joined, Suzanne Marquette's leave-taking from them appears to have been the best, considered from the point of view of both the tactics they employed and the caution she exhibited.

When she told the leader of the rural commune to which she belonged of her doubts and desires nearly two years into her stay, his response was not what she'd expected. He said, "You should leave if you feel that way. I disagree with you but I can respect your feelings." She was surprised and pleased. There was no spelled-out timetable for her leaving the Unification Church, and, indeed, she wasn't completely sure that she was going to go. Sensing her uncertainty, the group understandably tried to bolster her bond with them.

She noticed a clear increase in her companionship, and an intensification of the group's encouragement to participate. But once the seeds of doubt are sown, the harvest of homecoming seems to be inevitable. In all instances I have seen, there is an inexorable move outward matched with just as inexorable a loss of emotional investment in the group. Although the Moonies surrounded Suzanne with love, her yearning for home increased. Perhaps the five-week campaign of reconversion had to fail before her fellows could give it up, or perhaps it was merely a matter of form and the leader knew from the outset what the outcome would be. In any event, as suddenly as the pressure had been put on Suzanne, it was as abruptly removed. Again the leader told her that she was free to go and, as she had always believed, he was a man of his word. She was then left alone, though not shunned.

Yet Suzanne didn't leave immediately. The decision was clearly her problem; the Moonies had, so to speak, abdicated. Even after she phoned her parents to tell them of her decision to leave, she couldn't tell them when to expect her. It seemed that every time she came close to leaving, she had a change of heart. This competent young woman was not an indecisive person, but no matter which alternative she considered, whether she left or whether she stayed, the result was going to be difficult for her. The Unification Church had given her a new life and a happy one; she had eaten, slept, worked, and played their way among dear friends who had never done her ill. Yet to stay with less than the enthusiasm that had lighted their finest moments together was in itself a betrayal. But, again, going home was bound to rekindle painful feelings she recalled enduring in the months before her skating audition. But then—the decision seemed to circle endlessly—she had fond recollections of home. She vacillated in this way for another six weeks before finally saying good-by to her Moonie friends and hello to her waiting family.

The vacillation that Suzanne endured, with all its load of longing, guilt, doubt, and uncertainty, foreshadows what all these radical departers face in greater or lesser degree when their decision is finally made and they find themselves back where they started, home again. For in fact they have merely spiraled, though with increasing inner strength, back to the point of their departure: separation from parents and the inauguration of adulthood. All the fears and failures that had prevented them from taking a more direct path at the outset now come back to trouble them as they arrive at the point of departure again via their unusually circuitous route.

7
The Return

Philip Holtzman returned home almost twenty-two months to the day since the warm autumn evening of his departure into the yeshiva. Until nagging questions about the yeshiva and compelling images of home began to invade his thoughts, he had experienced a happiness more complete than any he had known. That sense of fulfillment, of spiritual lift, lingered in spite of doubts, so that when he was at last able to make the decision to go home, it was with a heavy heart.

The gap that may exist between parents and child at this point is well illustrated by Phil's phone call to his parents to tell them of his decision. The Holtzmans, as Dr. Holtzman had remarked, were still in "despair" about what had happened, and though they had picked up the threads of their own lives, Phil had not forgiven the many months of their unrestrained animosity. He had remained on guard, openly angry and still abusive. Glimmers of homesickness now were only that: a dim light at the end of a long tunnel. Yet to his parents, the news of his homecoming was the end of the tunnel—broad daylight, brilliant and wonderful. His news was greeted by his mother and father with tears of joy, exclamations of excitement, protestations of love.

Phil felt only disgust at this display. Worse, his parents said nothing during the telephone call about the yeshiva, and he was deeply disappointed. It was as though what had been to him the most important event in his life had never happened. He hung up determined to show them the true depth of his commitment to Judaism.

The Holtzmans happily prepared for Phil's homecoming. Their prayers had been answered; they would not lose their son to God after all. They were not unaware of the paradox in this; they had prayed against religion, even against God in a sense. To celebrate their son's return, they arranged a party. Yet, although they felt certain this was the appropriate way to welcome him, anticipation merged with apprehension. They feared a scene, the sort of ranting Phil had so often burdened them with in the last months. And they worried about whether he would be "presentable," the Phil of old, or the sallow, side-locked creature his friends had reported seeing on their abortive mission to Jerusalem.

His parents were somewhat reassured when Phil stepped off the plane in Denver seemingly in good physical shape. His curling side locks were shorn, though he wore a skullcap still. But he could not smile. The moment they had so often imagined, the joyful return of the prodigal son, eluded them.

The party also was not what they had hoped for. Phil didn't embarrass them, but he failed to gratify them either. He had great difficulty making small talk. He found the crowd of friends and relatives offensive. His discomfort was visible. "I wanted to scream 'You heathens!' " Phil later confided to me. "But something stopped me. Still, I thought I had made a terrible mistake by coming back."

Although the Holtzmans now began to sense the distance there was between their own experience and that of their child, to the extent that they apologized for the party the next day, they were unprepared for how wrenching a path their son had still to travel. Dr. Holtzman, hoping for a semblance of normalcy right from the start, was eager for Phil to enroll for the fall semester at the University of Colorado. There is that feeling in all of us: If we can get things to look all right on the outside, they will become all right on the inside too. Quite often this is true, but the turmoil inside Phil was beyond what his parents imagined. He didn't go to school that fall. The warnings of the zealous rabbi were loud in his mind. He was a sinner, he concluded; this was his retribution. He had condemned himself to a life of evil among nonbelievers. Feelings of worthlessness, which had vanished during his nearly two years in Jerusalem, now descended on him with almost unbearable weight and, he was sure, with deserved vengeance. He was indecisive, not only about important things, such as reentering college for his junior year and, at last, declaring his major, but also about trivial matters of everyday life, whether to go out or stay home, wear slacks or shorts, read this book or that one. Insomnia gripped him, and his parents were shocked to see that he could barely eat.

Recognizing the symptoms of depression, Mrs. Holtzman hoped to convince Phil to see a psychiatrist, but at that point she might as well have suggested a witch doctor. Still deeply tied to the yeshiva, even the temple he now attended with his parents felt to him like a heathen environment.

He heard about an Orthodox rabbi who ran a *shteeble*, a small, storefront synagogue, where he hoped to find relief. The rabbi welcomed him, but made it clear that he did not admire Phil's return to secular life. He advised him to return to the yeshiva. That decision too was beyond him.

It may be that the indecisiveness so typical during the first months of a radical departer's return is a blessing, since vacillation gives them breathing space and prevents impulsive choices. Instead of yielding to the pull of religious devotion, Phil consented to see a counselor known to the Orthodox Jewish community.

Many religious groups keep a listing of therapists whom they feel to be respectful of their beliefs, and youngsters like Phil who have only partially emerged from an intense religious experience tend to find such practitioners congenial to their needs. The counselor did not, for example, consider Phil's commitment to be a subject for probing, but instead helped him to place religion in a more helpful context. He reassured Phil that it was possible to live in the secular world and still be true to his spiritual convictions and practices. Supported by such perspectives, the Holtzmans were able to conform to Phil's dietary requirements, and he was able to expand his intellectual interests beyond the study of Torah and Talmud.

As the fall gave way to winter, Phil began to feel he had some control over his life. He registered for courses toward a major in life sciences for the spring term at the University of Colorado and chose to live in residence there rather than at home. To his own surprise, he was soon pricked with a genuine interest in his courses and became able to work with increasing zest in psychology and biology as well as comparative religion. The more involved in his studies he became, the less often he remembered to pray and the more frequently he found reasons not to make his weekly visit to the *shteeble*. Although his former relationship with his girlfriend was not rescuable, he fell in love with a girl he met at the university. Toward the end of his junior year, Phil took off his skullcap.

Parents who, like the Holtzmans, come to rapprochement only after prolonged bitterness and with extreme reluctance may be ill prepared for their child's return. As Phil noticed, they may behave as though nothing had happened; they bury their despair at the cost of burying the validity of their child's experience. They themselves have failed to appreciate that their child's destiny and their own are not the same.

Without a modicum of disinvolvement on the family's part, the returning child has difficulty maintaining the distance he now requires. Phil had defined that distance at least tentatively to himself. His hope was to go to medical school someday and become a doctor (just like his father), but he wished to remain a deeply observant Jew (unlike either of his parents). He tried to maintain that medium distance over his first months home by living with his family but at the same time criticizing the materialistic way in which their life was conducted. This distance his parents at first could not accept. They crowded him, when he needed space; hoped he hadn't changed, when he required acknowledgment of his difference.

But even when parents have been able to achieve a workable separation from their child, there is still a yawning gulf between them and a radical departer during the first weeks after the return. Whereas during the departure the burden of psychological work was clearly on the parents, now their task is largely over and it is the child's turn to undergo the wrenching work of separation.

For all these young men and women, their return, greeted with such relief and joy by their parents, is, for them, the ultimate ordeal they had been putting off so long. The self-disgust, disinterest, and uncertainty that had plagued them before their departure reappear, and now other feelings—depression and guilt—surface too. Parents, harangued for months or years by their apparently stridently secure and avowedly happy son or daughter, are caught off guard by the visibly confused and obviously unhappy child who arrives so suddenly on their doorstep.

This was particularly so with Jennifer Green, whose expulsion from the Healing Workshop had followed by a mere twenty-six hours her first admission of doubt. The last the Greens had heard from her before her return was a ringing endorsement of her way of life, her plan to move from Taos to the Bay Area in California to start a new Healing Workshop commune, and the usual condescending digs about their life style. She appeared at home in Houston one morning without announcement eleven months after her departure.

Mr. and Mrs. Green were thrilled, and dismayed, and desperately worried. Jennifer was extremely upset, and, although relieved to be home, was unable to confide her recent experience to her parents. They worried that something terrible might have happened to her. Mrs. Green in the months since Jennifer had left had become understandably cynical about the whole human-potential movement, but she recognized that her daughter was really in trouble now and would need outside help.

At the suggestion of still another therapy, Jennifer bristled at once. But her life was so painful that she did not hold out for long. Guilt assailed her on every side. She was haunted by thoughts of how she had hurt her parents and had given up the piano, and also of how she had abandoned her friends in the commune and betrayed its healing principles. The more she turned these thoughts over and over in her mind, the more confused she became. Her nights were filled with nightmares, and she awoke early, tired and listless, disinterested in friends or music, seldom hungry enough to eat a full meal.

Since Allen Green had assumed control some months before, he was no longer willing to let his wife and daughter resume the pattern that had seemed "crazy" to him for years, nor did Linda Green trust herself to make a wise choice of therapy at this point. Relying on Mr. Green's judgment, all three consulted a social worker trained in family therapy, whom they saw together once a week for the next six months. Family therapy is quite different from the reassurance and advice Phil received, and also from the more probing individual therapy some returning members require. Each member of the family is encouraged to articulate his or her own perspective of their relationship with each of the others—not confrontationally or with critical accusations, but merely as a statement of the meaning events have had for them. The result is a dawning of understanding: What one intends is not necessarily what the other perceives.

Patterns within the family change as members become more aware of how to serve others' needs in ways more in keeping with what they can accept and utilize. Still, changing perspectives takes time, and Jennifer was slower to face the realities of her position than her parents were to see in what ways they had played a part in family difficulties.

At first Jennifer could only cheer herself by fantasizing a miraculous recovery. She would be well again soon, nimbleness and surety would flow back into her unpracticed fingers and she would go to Julliard, become a concert pianist, meet a handsome hero, lead a fairytale existence. In short, she behaved as though the "time out" of her departure had not occurred in real time, as though she could pick up the thread of her life at just the moment of her departure.

This is one of the harsh realities of radical departures. Real time *is* lost, and for some it cannot be made up. So long a time without practice had left Jennifer far too rusty to entertain the thought of an audition. No conservatory of international stature would have touched her. She was not to become a concert pianist.

That year had, however, given this girl a chance to rearrange herself in a psychological sense. Whereas before she and her mother had been "as one," there was now a distance created by their criticism of one another and stabilized by their agreement to disagree. Across that distance they now looked at each other anew and almost at once found their way to a warm and loving relationship. Mr. Green played a part in this; so did the social worker. Both, by firmly insisting on a pragmatic view of how things were, rather than how one might wish them to be, intruded valuable perspective. Jennifer gained the strength to be grateful to her mother for never having severed their bond completely, even when, as she now recalled with horror, she had become so arrogant and spiteful.

As if in expression of that bond between two separate but loving people, she applied to the University of Texas in Austin for a double major: psychology and music.

For Jennifer and for all these returning young men and women there are fences to mend outside the immediate family too. But it is hard. What can returning members say to old friends whom they have so recently raked with criticism? How do they justify their leave-taking to neighbors who have been commiserating with their parents? Are they to apologize to the lover they left behind? Sometimes there has been a sad event—the death of Nancy Lewis's grandfather was one—to which the departer's response had been perfunctory or he did not respond at all. Neglect, antagonism, and ingratitude during the years of departure are not forgotten simply because the person now chooses to come home.

Toward all these people, the returning person feels enormous guilt. But the guilt stems from how the former member treated people, not from the departure itself. At most, they say that if they had it to do over again, they would have handled their radical departure differently—more gently, less suddenly, and with more careful explanations—but they do not feel that joining itself was a mistake. Indeed, they remain critical of society and, inevitably, of those who participate in it. That criticism, so necessary to their sense of being distinct and different from others, tends to boomerang. Jennifer and many others have told me that they felt "watched" upon their return, as though, in retribution for a series of unpardonable acts, they were to receive the public humiliation of exposure, scrutiny, and criticism.

How is such terrible guilt ameliorated? Time, of course, fades remorse, but the best reassurance for a child that his acts are forgivable is the fact that his parents are still intact. Mr. and Mrs. Green's ability finally to rise above the disaster of their daughter's radical departure, to renew their interest in other matters and in each other, paved the way for Jennifer's restitution within the family.

Remorse over betraying the group and fear of their criticism are not so easily soothed. The former member may be reluctant to talk about the group at all, and parents also may be uncomfortable in recalling that time, partly in fear of precipitating a painful reaction, or worse, a return to the group. The group may have used threats of retribution as a way of holding on to its members, as the zealous rabbi did with Phil. The more intolerant the group has been to its departing member, the greater the difficulty in readjusting to life in the outside world and the more likely that professional help will be needed.

Nancy Lewis, whose reaction to being "blissed" by the Children of God was literally to run from them in fear that they were after her, had a dreadful time for the first six months. Alternately angry and sad, she cried easily, pouted often, and withdrew from her family. She felt terrible about what she had done to her parents; yet she was just as miserable about abandoning her friends in the group. Visions of almost hallucinatory intensity flashed through her mind: she was there again, she could hear the songs exactly and feel former feelings as though they were happening now.

As is true of others who have been assailed with such flashbacks, this sense of being transported into the group again is not a soothing remembrance of days gone by, but a deeply unsettling experience from which the person emerges in a state verging on panic. Nancy was distraught over her own inability to control her sense of where she was, or to anchor herself in present time. Worse, these visions were so real that she was filled with terror that those one-time friends would turn on her at any moment.

In such a state, it was so impossible for her to concentrate on everyday matters that the Lewises found her as unable to participate in the household now as she had been unwilling to participate in her "grande artiste" days before her departure. Nor did that previous fantasy seem to serve her upon her return. Nancy would tell people of her plan to enter an excellent drama school, but she was so visibly agitated when she spoke of it that listeners felt uncomfortable. She couldn't sleep, couldn't eat; the mirror showed her a haggard face that she could barely recognize.

More than fifty percent of former members of radical groups show signs of emotional upheaval severe enough to warrant treatment during the first few months after their return. Of these, about a quarter are seen by a psychiatrist, psychologist, counselor, or social worker upon their return. For those who consider the possibility and who can overcome suspicion about the means and motives of therapists, even a rather brief opportunity to confide in a neutral outsider can speed their recovery, as was true for Phil and Jennifer. Nancy is an example of a returner in need of longer, more intensive therapy, a young woman who might not have been able to recover fully without it.

Nancy, like Jennifer and Phil, was reluctant at first to see a "shrink," as she called any psychotherapist. But her pain got the better of her, and she found herself approaching her mother with the query, "You know that shrink you spoke to me about a few weeks ago?" The therapist was one of the many Mrs. Lewis had contacted during her frantic days of searching out any expert at all, and the only one who, instead of dispensing a psychological "prescription," had listened while the Lewises spilled out their confusion. She was an M.D. and a psychiatrist accustomed to the complexities that careful listening is more likely to reveal than is textbook psychology. She had given the Lewises no pat answers to what to "do" about Nancy while she was committed to the Children of God, but did help them to get through their mourning and what appeared to be the incipient breakup of their marriage. They appreciated her willingness to hear them out, and felt that Nancy would be comfortable with her. She was to see Nancy alone, and without the reports to parents that might be appropriate with a younger person.

She was not what Nancy expected. Nancy had built up a fantasy of what the psychiatrist, her office, and the session would be like. Instead of an austere, impersonal place, their meetings took place in comfortable upholstered chairs in an informal, warm setting that was, in fact, a wing of the doctor's home. Instead of a reserved, removed, and intellectual older woman, Nancy discovered a charming, giving woman in her early forties. And in place of uncomfortable monologue broken only by interpretive pronouncements from her psychiatrist—

accusations, Nancy had thought they would be—there was give-and-take conversation, humor and sharing.

Nancy had anticipated that her fears and nightmares would be the "target" symptoms, that they would spend some time talking about her experiences with the Children of God, and that, after a few weeks of twice-weekly sessions, all would be well. That was only partly so. Intense stress reactions—fear, insomnia, lack of appetite, flashbacks—tend to disappear within a few weeks of treatment, and did with Nancy. But she herself knew that they had barely begun to explore whatever had been pushing her from pose to pose for all the years since childhood.

They talked about her experiences in the Children of God, but their sessions went far afield from there. They traveled back to times well before her radical departure. They let light fall on her aspirations, found and refitted many pieces of how she as a child had felt about her parents, and, most important, dared to look at how she viewed herself.

Gradually, Nancy began to lay out the brushstrokes of a modified view. She neither needed the bravado of the "grande artiste," the great Sarah Bernhardt, with the world at her feet, who looked on her peers as peons, nor did she need to be a perfectly good child, a Child of God. A realistic perception of herself as a warm, emotional, modestly talented young woman emerged. This trimmed-to-reality view had the smack of genuineness missing before—enough goodness to feel good about, not so much badness after all.

Nancy came to see her previous going around with a bad crowd as a sort of despair at ever being much good, of taking drugs as a way of not looking at how awful she thought she was, and at joining the Children of God as a way of not having any failings at all. By the time she could see herself as imperfect but nevertheless likable and worthy, she no longer had to blame her parents for being "carriers of the ills of society," germs that had infected her in the days when any failings of theirs were diseases of herself. Her relationship with her parents improved, and this lent additional support to her work to become a person she could like.

This is not to say that therapy was easy. There were times when Nancy was in tears confronting some fact about herself that she didn't like or losing some defense that had comforted her in the past. On several occasions, she did not want to keep appointments, and disparaged her therapist. Intensive therapy at its best, however, proves its worth by real-world measures of improved performance, relationships, and inner ease. These were enough in the nine months of Nancy's treatment to encourage her persistence in spite of inevitable pain.

By the end of that time, she developed an interest that was altogether startling to her family. She enrolled in a business course at a local junior college, determined to learn her way around the world of commerce represented by her father, the rug salesman, who, Nancy had once sarcastically claimed, measured her worth in dollars and cents.

Not all children go through these months of depression and confusion after their return. Suzanne Marquette, whose leaving of the Moonies had come about only after several months of vacillation, fitted back into home life as into a comfortable pair of shoes. Even she was surprised. It may be that she had done some of the work of readjustment before she left. One might predict that children who do not leave the group impulsively, whose group tolerates a prolonged leave-taking and finally accepts it without rancor, have a better prognosis for a happier return. But it is also true that Suzanne's mother had kept those "care packages" coming, no matter what, and that both the Marquettes, in contrast especially to Phil's parents, treaded gingerly into the unknown of their daughter's return.

The Marquettes had received numerous calls from Suzanne while she was grappling with her wish to leave the Moonies. Though she talked about her intention to come home, she could not say when. Therefore her parents were allowed to participate in her conflict and themselves to feel wary about the outcome. They also had time to arm themselves for the worst, based on advice from former members' families and discussions of the forthcoming return with a psychiatrist who stood ready to help if necessary. When the moment came, it was not celebrated with a homecoming party; instead, emotions were muted, as though the actual return, so long awaited, were an anticlimax.

The Marquettes' worst fears weren't realized. Suzanne began seeing old friends within weeks; it took only two weeks before she was back on the ice and was again giving skating lessons to her delighted brothers. It may well be that a tentative stance on the parents' part allowed

Suzanne herself to choose the distance that was most comfortable for her, whereas displays of intense feeling might have inflicted too much closeness too soon. At any rate, she did not experience that typical feeling of being torn between two worlds. She felt the need neither to criticize the Moonies with whom she had been so happy for almost two years, nor to despise herself for having hurt her family. Her sense of balance was demonstrated also in her plans for herself. She no longer had aspirations to reach the "top" as a skater, though she still enjoyed skating very much. She went back to junior college, filled with plans to continue on into social work or some branch of the ministry. Family and friends could see this real change. Over and over, they noticed a "spiritual" quality in Suzanne, as well as glowing health and genuine happiness.

Jamie Gould's experience was similar, and for similar reasons. He too had had a long period in which to discuss with friends in the Church of Scientology their mutual doubts during the period of their group's internal crisis. Those many conversations, and also public preoccupation with the group's turmoils, focused his thoughts on what he would do once outside the group and what his future might be like. Moreover, he did not leave alone; his leave-taking was modeled on the departure of others who had enjoyed considerable esteem within the group before allying themselves on the side of doubt. Nor for Jamie was there a physical move away from the protected commune out into the glare of the world or the ordeal of an overemotional homecoming. He had continued to live in his house. Julia lived there with him; she agreed with his reasons for leaving, and left the group at the same time. They simply continued to live with each other, and married three months after their return to the outside world.

Given time to work out his feelings, support for his ultimate decision, and the maturity he had gained through his relationship with Julia, Jamie left the church feeling strong and sure about his choice. There was little ambivalence. He had gotten what he could from the group and, though it was no longer for him, he had no reason to condemn it. He couldn't say whether the charges against their leader, L. Ron Hubbard, were valid; this and other matters of public debate quickly became beside the point as he took strides to control his own life.

For Jamie, the oldest of these radical departers, rapprochement with his parents never really came about. But neither had there been any peak of anger, bitterness, and despair. Unlike the Holtzmans, who felt they had lost the most promising of their three children, Jamie's parents had for many years felt an aching disappointment in him, and his joining neither worsened nor bettered the distance they had already put between them. Perfunctory calls from the Bahamas and from the Riviera continued, yet even in years to come no real progress was made between the Goulds and their younger son.

Julia in many ways filled the gap. With her, Jamie was able to find a degree of intimacy reliable enough to replace both his longing for closeness with his parents and his substitute union with the Church of Scientology. By marrying her, he declared at least a formal separation from his parents. And Julia herself sought rapprochement with the Goulds during the months between their leaving the group and their marriage. Largely through her influence, John Gould, whose currency of love had for so long been actual cash, nevertheless was able to use that avenue to celebrate his son's severance from the group in a way that was very helpful. He promised to set him up in whatever sort of business Jamie desired. While working in the Scientology bookstore, the young man had become intrigued with the world of bookselling. He loved browsers and buyers alike, enjoyed the pace of the business, and had an intelligent grasp of its financial structure. He was ready with a plan when his father made his offer. Using his father's capital, Jamie opened a small bookstore in a pleasant university area of New York City. That store was an immediate success, and Jamie has never looked back.

Fred Vitelli, after taking his time about leaving the anarchist Armed Guard, did not take up his life where he had left it eighteen months earlier. Instead, he returned a better person, giant steps ahead of where he had been at the time of his radical departure.

Fred's breaking away had proved particularly helpful. To this boy who had been so uncertain of what deserved his anger that he had flung it indiscriminately at everyone, the Armed Guard had given a just target. This newly focused anger was not to be destructive; it was to build a better world, one of which Fred and all others would no longer have cause to complain. One can imagine the pleasure in such a graduation. The young tough on the loose in Rome was like an enraged infant who can only bawl his discomfort. The twenty-one-year-old who returned home had learned the value of directing aggressiveness to the correction of his own and others' discomforts. This pleasure must be felt to some degree by all these committed members as they turn from what has seemed futile battles to march with their righteous armies.

There were several other sources of Fred's pleasure. One was that his railing at everyone else's "bullshit" masked a degree of self-hatred that was withering. Hating capitalism, Marxism, war, and injustice is much more comfortable, especially if you're the hero come to eradicate these evils. Also, by joining in group anger, the member can disavow his own personal gripes. Hostility no longer felt personal to Fred; it was moral outrage that emanated from his group's cause and therefore transcended individual responsibility.

Thus relieved of self-hatred, personal gripes about his fellows, and even of responsibility for aggressiveness, Fred found a real emotional safety within the Armed Guard. The members all took aim in unison at targets beyond themselves, and were therefore safe in friendship with one another. Fred left home a lion; he returned a lamb.

Anthony and Maria Vitelli were not only delighted to have Fred home again, but also quickly noticed the change in him. He, once so snide, self-centered, and superficial that it was hard to like him, had turned serious. Anticipating problems, his mother at first interpreted this sober attitude as depression, but after they had spent a few days together she realized that her son had shed thick layers of bravado, cynicism, and arrogance. His sincerity was real. Yet Fred's new-found sincerity illustrates particularly well another problem that plagues radical departers when they first return to their former lives. Like Phil's, his most heartfelt intentions came packaged in doubts. Whatever decision he considered culminated in indecision. Were his motives pure? Was this the right choice? He would answer himself affirmatively, then more tentatively, and then qualify his thought, modify it somewhat, change his mind—answer negatively. It was as though, serious as he had become, sincerity required him continually to question and distrust his own judgment. For every decision there was a doubt, for every yes a no, and the result was that it took him some months to recommit himself to anything.

One can guess several reasons why former joiners might experience this painful indecisiveness upon their return. For many—and that certainly includes Fred, who had been so feckless and enmeshed in fantasy—their radical departure had been the first major decision of their lives, and that decision had culminated in doubt. More than that, their sense of having a worthy self is still tentative and is nearly drowned in guilt. They can't afford to make still more mistakes, because any new failing heaped upon what they see as years of wrongdoing would sink them completely. This is particularly so with senior members who have risen by virtue of their zeal to lieutenants or comparable members of the inner circle. They above all others in the group and for the longest period of time have anchored their self-esteem in the rightness of their cause. To leave, either because of their own doubting or because the group disbands, is to place their judgment and their selfhood in serious jeopardy.

And there is another reason returning members are so indecisive. For a year or more every detail of their lives has been decided for them— what to wear, read, eat; when to work and sing and sleep; whom to befriend and whom to distrust; what the answers are. What's more, every member of the group had acted and thought along the same lines exactly. When they come home, everything is ambiguous. Few families have anything remotely resembling the martialed life of the group. There are as many opinions as there are people; no family has the answers. Overwhelmed by choice, any one of which could be a wrong one, it seems safest to make no choice at all.

Yet the fact is that Fred, Jamie, Phil, Jennifer, Suzanne, and Nancy all had made the choice to come home. The more that choice appears to be right because life within the family really is made comfortable for them and people really are glad to welcome them back, the more easily can they shoulder again the responsibility of making decisions for themselves.

Fred, in fact, had a relatively easy time of it. His peers, who used to have to listen to tirades of put-downs and one-upmanship, were in-

credulous. Fred was warm, eager to hear what others had to say, concerned—all attributes he had so well hidden before his departure.
Surrounded now by family and friends, he found it natural to enjoy
their company and, over the weeks, to begin again to exercise judgment. No longer the brash exploiter who "had it made" in his father's
business, he now looked forward to going to college, to studying political science, and perhaps—such things seemed possible now—eventually to pursuing a legal or political career.

There is a widely held belief that once a young person is "hooked" on
the radical life style of one of these groups, an ordinary life in the outside world is no longer possible. Should the person leave one group
for whatever reason, goes the belief, he or she will quickly join another. "Cult-hopping" is, in fact, a rarity. Only about two to three
percent of radical departures are ever repeated in another group. Yet
this is exactly what happened to Kathy O'Connor.

When Kathy left the Divine Light Mission after the unseemly de-
posing of the Maharaj Ji, she had been there for over three years. Unlike most other radical departers, her doubts sprang only from her sense
that this group had betrayed her; her uneasiness was not accompanied
by those unbidden longings for home or, in her case, for her husband,
Michael. Therefore she did not return either to him or to her family.
She remained in New Orleans and again took up her occupation as a
nurse.

But this was in no way "life as usual." Whereas other former
members enact their guilt within their families—and feel guilt about
them—Kathy felt no regrets about either Michael or her mother and
father. She lived alone—or almost. For she was accompanied always
by the now-malignant presence of the deposed Maharaj Ji. She believed his magical spirit had the power to hurt her and felt bereft of
defense against his imagined fury. This extreme fear is not usual, but
it is sometimes seen in those who have left zealous groups that thrive
on seeing "the enemy" everywhere. Sometimes the fear is impersonal,
as when Phil feared some vague retribution from his deity for the sin
of returning to the heathen world. But as often the fear is personal—
and it may be real. Former joiners are convinced that the members

they left behind, the "betrayed" ones, might seek vengeance on them, the "traitors." Since this has really happened—for example, to defectors from the People's Temple in California and later in Guyana—former members of zealous, threatening groups are often reluctant to share any information about their former comrades or to talk about life within the group.

Kathy was such a one. Her fear isolated her and prevented her from finding in the outside world the protection, psychological and physical, that was found by the other young people discussed here. Given both her feeling of being in imminent danger and her disdain for worldly concerns, she could not go on living a life devoid of transcendent belief and intense belonging. Within three months, she was a committed member of the Sri Chinmoy, a group similar in mystic style and Indian leadership to the group she had so recently left.

Her story illustrates the fact that leaving a group and making an actual return are not the same thing. Return is marked by a determination, however painful and filled with ambivalence, to resolve relationships with the family, usually within the former setting. In my experience, if there is no homecoming in either a physical or an emotional sense, the probability is that the joiner who has left a group is merely "between jobs" and has not set for himself the task of resolution. Kathy and others like her live on as long-term members of a group self, unable to establish their separate identity, although they may adopt one group identity after another. Unlike the resolution ultimately sought by most former members, those who only move from group to group have resolved not to resolve, at least for the time being.

There are also young men and women who stay in the group but who do continue their personal growth. At the time of this writing, Dennis Ericson has been with 3HO for fourteen years. When President Jimmy Carter pardoned draft dodgers in 1971, Dennis began to visit his family in San Diego regularly, and Jack Ericson, that old army man and no-nonsense conservative, began to visit the 3HO commune in Vancouver. There he found not the garrison mentality he expected, and which is so usual in these groups, but open, gentle young people who worked hard for a living in their various enterprises, helped others through courses and retreats but did not proselytize, and were clean, neat, healthy, and relaxed. Mr. Ericson became friends with some of the members.

During visits home, Dennis convincingly expressed his sense of commitment to a "higher calling." To him, materialism and competitiveness would never have allowed him to be as useful to others as he now was. His father began to read about the group's beliefs and didn't find its precepts as threatening as he had expected. Although Ivy and Jack Ericson feel even now that Dennis would have been better off entering a profession, they have admitted that his way of life makes more and more sense to them.

3HO is, of course, an unusual group in that it conducts itself within society—though perhaps off to one side. Dennis's convictions never escalated into outright hostility toward his parents' way of life. At the time when he might have had to wrench himself from the group by torturing doubts and abrupt disillusionment in order to return to his family, he was able simply to exchange visits with them much as might any young man who has established himself as a separate person by earning his way at some distance from home. Finding that path to growing up is no different from choosing to become, say, an artist when one's family disdains the world of art. The bohemian life seems dangerously on the fringe to many people. Dennis's and his parents' experience demonstrates that the terrible pain wrought by a radical departure is caused by the rift between the child and his family, and not necessarily by the nature of the beliefs that the child espouses. When the rift is repaired, parents can see the group itself in a new light.

This story also points up the fact that the groups vary widely in their effect on their members. Even a group as gentle and nonintrusive as 3HO affected some young people and their families negatively. The Ericsons happened to be taken by the philosophy and impressed with their son's life—albeit guardedly. I could just as easily have selected another set of parents of a member of the same group who felt that 3HO was repulsive and destructive, and who ensured that a painful schism resulted from their antagonism.

A few radical departers stay with the group they joined not because they are able to use it in a true resolution of their problems, but because any resolution at all has been cut off by the brutality of their parents' response. Ethan Browning's experience was such a catastrophe.

"A Browning doesn't quit" was the family's motto, and both father and son subscribed to it. They quickly reached a mutually embittered impasse. With neither side willing to compromise—to agree to disagree—there was no way to bridge the gulf between them. To do so would have seemed capitulation.

Ethan's leaders in the Hare Krishna had explained his family's hostility: their antagonism was a reflection of their own decadence and corruption. He must be on his guard against them, they told Ethan, because parents like his could not be trusted and were capable of anything. When the time came, less than a year after his joining, that Ethan began to doubt the purity of the group, he wanted to discuss this opening up of his thoughts with his father, but Stuart Browning's brick-walled antagonism made this impossible. Patricia Browning, drinking heavily, was pretty much out of the picture. Ethan was backed into a corner.

Ethan's father was intransigent. He was a man in whom frustration and impotence smoldered and then flamed into towering anger. He spoke in tough terms. He was used to playing hardball and winning. He was damned if he was going to let a bunch of freaks make a fool of him. He'd do anything to shake Ethan up, to snap him out of this nonsense, to get him away from this bunch of kooks. "If I could have bombed their temple," this upright Episcopalian told me in so many words, "or killed their leaders without getting caught, I would have done it, believe me."

Unable to bear frustration any longer, Mr. Browning hired a deprogramer, who charged $8,000 plus expenses for the "job," as he called it. The deprogramer was a fundamentalist Christian who worked with his wife to "return Christian kids back to the fold." An appointment with Ethan was arranged by subterfuge. Mr. Browning called his son at the Hare Krishna temple and told him he wanted to get together to patch up their difficulties. He even went so far as to say that perhaps he could learn something from Ethan about the Hare Krishna. Although wary, Ethan was inwardly delighted. He agreed to meet his father the same evening after prayers.

Mr. Browning picked Ethan up in his car outside the temple. They were immediately joined by two men and a woman who had been parked behind them. Ethan was visibly frightened in spite of his father's assurance that they were only there to help him. During the drive to an out-of-the-way lakeside bungalow rented out of season by the deprograming team, Mr. Browning could only repeat over and over, "We're going to help you."

Once Ethan was inside the bungalow, his father left almost immediately. The door was locked; deprograming began. For the next seventy-two hours Ethan was subjected to the only kind of brainwashing I have come upon during all my years of studying radical departures—that practiced by deprogramers.

The method is designed to whip away defenses. Ethan was subjected to shouted attacks on the leaders he revered, to scathing criticism of his belief, and to rude baring of its inconsistencies. He was baited and insulted into angry response, then ridiculed with laughter. At any sign that he was becoming helpless with anger—the quiver of his chin, tears—he was stabbed with guilt-inducing accusations. "Look what you've done to your mother," one of the threesome would insist, and he would be confronted with images of her grief and pain.

Then the assault would stop, abruptly at times, gradually at other times. A deprogramer might put a hand on Ethan's shoulder and offer sympathy and understanding; the boy was still only 16. "You must be tired," the woman would acknowledge. "We'll play soft music and you can sleep."

The respite might be three minutes; it might be an hour. Then Ethan would awaken to a blare of music turned to unendurable volume and the barrage would begin again. Breaks and attacks were random, so he couldn't anger himself for the next onslaught. Nor could he guard himself with the appropriate defense. The attacks shifted rapidly from intellectual barbs to emotional poisons.

He tried valiantly to withdraw behind a barricade of meditation, but prodding fingers and intrusive shouting made concentration impossible.

As the hours wore on, the deprogramers offered a new sort of respite: peaceful passages, quietly recited, from the familiar texts of the New Testament. They were ones any Christian child has memorized in Sunday school, and were redolent of a trusting childhood. It was at this point that Ethan broke down emotionally. He was by then exhausted, defenseless, and grateful for the planned regression that was now offered to him.

He listened, cooperated, agreed to what was asked of him. Blankly, he thanked his "protectors," as they called themselves. This is similar to the gratitude that hostages feel toward their tormentors at the height of their helplessness; brainwashing relies on the same victim psychology. Three days had passed. Ethan was declared free of his "affliction."

The Brownings were enormously pleased with how easily Ethan had given up his beliefs and were eager for me to see the results for myself immediately. Ethan agreed to a visit the morning after his deprograming; he knew me from our hours of interviewing within the Hare Krishna. At the time of our last talk, when he had been within his group for nine months, he had seemed somewhat rigid and serious, but still a personable and forthcoming young man. This time those large hazel eyes appeared sunk in dark sockets. I saw furtive glances, agitation, and pained discomfort that belied the pat and agreeable answers he gave to my remarks and questions. Ethan was in trouble, and I reflected this to him. I told him that I was pleased that he had come to see me and hoped that he would come again. He didn't come back; not to me, not to his family or to anyone outside of the Hare Krishna.

By the end of that day, Ethan had disappeared within the bowels of his group.

There is no doubt that the burden of anguish at the time of return falls upon the radical departer. His difficulties will be greater the more intolerant and threatening his group has been, the more unbridled his hostility toward his family, and the more abrupt his decision to come home. Yet, the possibility of return to the outside world also relies in many ways on how well parents have been able to cope with the original departure. Those parents who have maintained a bond with their child while accepting that there is distance and difference between them can expect their child, however painfully and slowly, to grow up like any other child.

Radical departures that fail to give the child strength to grow fail largely because parents themselves can't let go of their child enough for him to achieve perspective, or because the person is disturbed in other ways and not simply suffering from a delay in development. Ethan was ready to emerge from the Hare Krishna had anyone been prepared to receive him. Instead, his father severed the last shreds of his trust. Kathy too, though perhaps her fear of the Maharaj Ji verged on the pathological, might have fared better had her family recognized that this was the moment to step back into her life. None of the nine young men and women looked at here could be considered disturbed in a psychiatric sense, and six of them returned home and made a full recovery within only a few years from what seemed, at first, a frightening departure from normal life.

There is a small percentage of joiners who are troubled or disturbed beforehand. For them, we cannot make reliable predictions.

It is not as simple as it might seem to say who was and who was not disturbed before their radical departure. A prior history of therapy isn't a reliable criterion, because some families don't seek therapy under any circumstances and others, like the Greens, enter treatment for even transient psychological discomfort. With that caveat, it can be said that, of the ten percent of joiners who had been in therapy before departure, those who appear normal after their return and those who appear to be disturbed are in about the same proportion as those who had undergone treatment in that age group in the general population. Statistically, at least, their destiny remains unaffected by their joining.

More can be learned clinically on a case-by-case basis through interview with joiners and their families. Certainly a trained clinician should be able to discover within several hours of conversation whether a person shows pathology at that time, but whether the individual was disturbed a year or more ago is still problematical. People tend to censor memory selectively to suit conclusions they have drawn. For example, Phil's parents assumed schizophrenia at the time of his joining and dredged from "memory" any hints of odd behavior that might suit that theory. The opposite could also be true: a family might relieve their sense of guilt by a kidnapping or brainwashing theory and paint their memories of their child with extraordinary normalcy. Joiners themselves can unconsciously distort their recollections in their own defense.

There is also the problem of what is considered pathological. These days the formal and informal vocabulary of mental illness is bandied about with little regard for its accuracy. Just as Jennifer was accused of being a psychopath, many casually accuse others of being "sick," neurotic, schizoid, paranoid, and so on when they really mean to disparage a personality trait they dislike in that person. Adolescence can be such a bumpy time emotionally that behavior often seems temporarily odd without its signifying pathology. An amazing number of teen-age girls shoplift, but one can't say they have a "character disorder"; bouts of depression are common, but they don't call for the label "depressive." One might not like the acting-out behavior of Nancy or Fred, and one might worry about Ethan's aloofness, but the future course of their lives indicates that they suffered a developmental crisis and not a neurosis.

Nevertheless, my experience shows that there are troubled youth whose radical departures don't "work" in the sense that they are unable to use them for their own internal growth, a frankly disturbed population that is vulnerable to a worsening of condition during membership in certain kinds of groups, and, surprisingly, some severely disturbed individuals whose condition is stabilized by joining.

The members I have interviewed who are unable to benefit from joining might be classed as runaways. They tend to be years younger than the majority of joiners; the youngest I have met are only fourteen or fifteen years old. They have not necessarily run away from home in the usual sense, but their joining a radical group has been their attempt to escape from what they perceive to be a destructive home environment. They are, as a group, troubled and overly susceptible to promises of simplistic answers to their problems. Some are actually chronic runaways or have been "on the road" for some time. These may be only seeking shelter and, although they may exploit the group for many months and even curb their streetwise behavior as a condition of membership, they don't experience commitment and remain emotionally aloof from their fellows.

Chronic runaways and the very young who seek escape from disruptive home lives seldom make any real inroads into their problems. What gains they make in improved behavior are superficial ones that they are unable to consolidate or to build upon when they return. Whether they are harmed by membership depends on the nature of the group. Capricious, intrusive, and abusive leadership—a few like Jim Jones have psychotic delusions of omnipotence—endangers all followers, and, most of all, those who have the least defense.

In general, an individual whose psychological balance relies heavily on rigid defenses is most vulnerable to confrontational groups, whose intrusive methodology strips members bare of defense. Unhappily, the majority of such groups advertise themselves as therapeutic and therefore attract—and fail to screen out—an unusually high proportion of just those people who may be harmed by them.

A frightening example was David Dubow, a graphic designer in his mid-20s. As a freshman in college, Dave suffered a period of intense panic and suspiciousness, for which he was successfully treated by counseling and medication. Since that episode, he had been able to keep panic at bay by obsessive attention to detail. Everything had to be just so in his apartment and in his work. Increasingly, his obsessiveness interfered with his getting his work done by deadlines, and he was fired from his job. Anxiety mounted, and he had the sense that people were against him and everything was getting out of control.

Dave joined the Inner Search Project (ISP), a therapeutic group whose technique is constant confrontation. Members are encouraged to shout criticisms at one another—hardly a good choice for someone who already feels persecuted. Dave's defenses gave way within three months and he had to be admitted to a psychiatric hospital in a state of crippling fear.

It is also true that less abusive groups who don't advertise themselves as therapeutic and from which others emerge without apparent damage may be damaging to some individuals. Usually there has been a prior history of continual seeking for magical solutions, each of which has been taken up with totally unrealistic expectations and, when the "cure" isn't immediately forthcoming, as quickly dropped. Jane Curtis, for example, had during adolescence and into her 20s tried to cure her recurrent depressions and almost uncontrolled obesity by private therapy, a Gestalt group, transcendental meditation, megavitamins, macrobiotic diet, and a stay at a health spa.

When Jane joined the Divine Light Mission—the same group Kathy O'Connor found so gratifying—she had just received the particularly crushing blow of a first love affair that had come to an abrupt and disillusioning end. Her magical hopes were dashed once again when her depression became even more acute after a single month in the group. Other members saw her crying often and fidgeting always. Distressed that she could not participate and recognizing the severity of her condition, the group was forced to take her to a hospital for treatment.

A problem in assessing the effect of the group on such joiners' mental condition is that there is no way to be sure whether their illness would have worsened anyway. For these vulnerable people whose hold over a sane and comfortable perception is tenuous at best, any stress at all is likely to constitute a risk.

But what constitutes stress? Surprisingly, I found in my work very disturbed individuals who escaped stress by their radical departure. One instance was a boy of 17 who was the tense and anxious product of an embattled marriage. He suffered from a host of somatic complaints, not only the usual bowel problems and a "knot in the stomach," but also profuse sweating, tics, tremors, and even blurred vision. Within months of joining an offshoot of the Jewish Defense League—certainly a distressing group to those outside it—all these anxiety symptoms disappeared.

Even a diagnosed schizophrenic can on occasion find relief in group membership. Most groups can recognize blatant psychosis and rarely accept a bizarre individual. If they can tolerate schizophrenic behavior, however, there is a chance that the member can fit in well. Alan Thompson, for example, was able to use a charismatic commune's strange rituals and idiosyncratic language to replace his own psychotic symptoms. The group's structure reduced choice, offered him a needed separation from society, and gave him simple, useful things to do. Alan was not, of course, "cured," but he functioned better within the group than outside it.

Because the emotional expressions and the intellectual functioning of members are so shallow and stereotyped while they are in the midst of commitment, it isn't possible to judge the effect a radical departure has had on a youth until his or her return. Judging from the first six months back at home, it's safe to say that a reassuring majority of former members have not been damaged by their departure, although the time they have lost from school or other goals may be irretrievable, some relationships may have suffered irrevocably, and the readjustment period is fraught with difficulties.

That small percentage that was clinically disturbed in the first place may still be disturbed, or may be worse, or may be better. There is as yet no evidence that these groups attract, predispose, or precipitate psychiatric disturbance any more than other demanding memberships—the armed services or medical school, for example—which society finds acceptable. (Ironically, the exception may be therapeutic groups, but hard data are so far insufficient to give any but an impressionistic judgment.) As for the very young, it's likely that they will be no better off, and may well be worse off, after their return than before their radical departure.

To say that nine out of ten children who make radical departures return within several years or less to pick up the threads of their lives successfully—and that the remaining one was perhaps as likely to have fared ill whether he joined or not—is not to say that one would wish a radical departure on anyone. Regardless of whether or not our children are able to utilize this peculiar time out, the pain families endure is excruciating, the child may be injured, and society is injured too. By understanding, however, what it is that joiners seek, why they find commitment gratifying, and in what ways the experience is of genuine psychological use to them, one is in a better position to judge what should be done.

Are there legal recourses for rescuing from their group at least the most vulnerable members? If there are not, should more effective legislation be sought? Most crucial, since a great deal has been learned about the critical period that precedes a radical departure and the nature of the solution children find for themselves, perhaps their crises can be alleviated before they are forced to break away, or, if they must break away, better alternatives be offered for belief and belonging.

Finally, it needs to be asked whether any sort of belief and belonging has anything but a transient effect on joiners. It needs to be known if Philip Holtzman was able to resolve his growing interest in medicine with his abiding faith in Orthodoxy, whether Nancy Lewis grew up to marry, have children, and enjoy the middle-class life she had once spurned, what becomes of cult-hoppers like Kathy, and whether deprogramed youngsters like Ethan Browning ever do emerge from their refuge within the group.

Radical departures point to particular difficulties within middle-class culture and to deficiencies in modern Western society as a whole. The children are only doing the best they can; it's up to adults to seek better resolutions in partnership with them.

8
Resolutions

A "worst case" analysis of radical departures would certainly reveal the sorts of atrocities that are covered from time to time in lurid detail by the media and have occasioned the loudest outcries that "something should be done" about these groups. I can add nothing from my own personal experience, but perhaps I can clarify how atrocities occur and assure readers again that they are exceedingly rare.

I have myself seen no suicide, murder, prostitution, starvation, torture, or brainwashing. Of those few members who suffer nervous breakdowns while committed to the group, any might have suffered breakdown under similar conditions of stress not unique to radical-group membership. Of those evidently normal kids who got more than they bargained for in the way of emotional upset, almost all were in groups that were unusually demanding, intrusive, and paranoid. Indeed, the most abusive groups are under the sway of a leader whom psychiatry would diagnose as psychotic or psychopathic—that is, delusional or without restraint of conscience.

During commitment, radical departers are unable to judge the worth or competence of their leaders. Their adulation emanates from their inner need to abrogate control to a "perfect master." His followers suspend critical judgment, become numb to conflict, and refuse to exercise personal choice. They narrow their emotional range by shutting down bad feelings; they feel euphoric, although the rest of us find them bland. They do the same intellectually. Joiners are incredibly narrow just when they feel their comprehension to be most expansive.

While in this self-induced state of mind, radical departers are totally vulnerable to whatever their leaders say they should think or do. When the leader is criminal or paranoid, the situation can easily get out of hand. Members' adulation feeds the scheming or self-aggrandizing delusions of the leader, so that the more he is revered and obeyed, the more grandiose and manipulative he may become. His grandiosity and power in turn excite his followers to even greater passion and eagerness to sacrifice themselves in his behalf. This spiraling intensity may be furthered when the group feels beleaguered by the outside world. Exalted paranoia grips them; the stage is set for catastrophe.

Perhaps it is gratuitous to remark that the combination of extreme adulation and monstrous requests is not exclusive to radical groups. The Inquisition, the Holocaust, and the My Lai massacre each resulted from a similar conspiracy of human failings. Also, at the cost of being glib, I will note that it has seemed to me that even disreputable leaders usually see more to gain from exploiting financial opportunities than from demanding crimes, and therefore in most cases venality can be trusted to obviate atrocity.

Even leaders who in their first flush of power overstep the limits of law generally learn to be more careful rather quickly. The Unification Church, which used heavy-handed recruitment tactics in its early days, treads more gently now. The Children of God's "happy hookers" are cautioned not to approach minors and not to charge money; they are therefore practicing neither statutory rape nor prostitution.

No matter what the avowed practices of the group or the potentially dangerous nature of its leader, actual practices of a particular unit and its leader may be quite different. The Reverend Moon entertains delusions of omnipotence and has been convicted of tax evasion, but the local leader of Suzanne Marquette's Moonie commune was a man of humility and integrity. Nancy Lewis knew about the happy-hooker tactic but was never asked to use it.

I strongly urge parents to visit the local group unit their child has joined to judge for themselves the personality of the leader and the character of his practices. Ordinary politeness and suspension of aggressive challenge will usually assure that the member's family is treated in kind. That was true when Stuart and Patricia Browning visited the Hare Krishna temple in the week before Ethan's final decision. They were treated graciously and allowed to watch everyday observances and activities. They were too ready, however, to pounce upon peculiarities rather than assess the emotional tenor within the temple.

Peculiarities are beside the point. If the local leader is gracious, accessible, kind, and sensitive, and if group conduct also appears gentle and caring, there is probably no realistic basis for alarm. The most benign groups, such as 3HO, never demand estrangement from parents, find other work for members uncomfortable with fund-raising, and use no subterfuge in their relations with the outside world. Coercion in such a group is no greater than the pressure to conform anybody might experience in, say, his place of business or his club. On the other hand, suspicion, hostility, aggressively intrusive meetings, and punishing confrontations should arouse parents' vigilance.

Although children are for the most part safe within their groups, the situation can change, as it apparently did in the People's Temple over a period of only a few years. Former members and survivors have documented the evolution of paranoia and aggressiveness from what originally had been a relatively benign atmosphere before the Temple found itself under attack from the outside world. The Unification Church during a period of public criticism responded with grandiose and risky plotting in which some members were involved. According to the report of a former member, one scheme required a squad of devotees to rush through the Secret Service guards at the White House tree-lighting ceremony one Christmas and hoist President Richard Nixon on their shoulders to demonstrate the power of Moonie "support." Individual members may also undergo onerous physical or emotional changes that are independent of what is happening within the group as a whole.

Therefore I also urge parents to maintain communication and to visit when possible to check things out all during their child's stay. One young member I knew was so carried away by his own faith that he decided he could do without his insulin injections for juvenile-onset diabetes. This was not a group belief, but his own interpretation of the power of faith. Discovering what had happened, the boy's parents were able to talk it over with the group leader, who agreed to insist on proper medical care.

Fred Vitelli might also have put himself in physical danger through terrorist exploits. Terrorist groups present a special problem because of their secrecy, but studied ingenuousness on parents' part could conceivably result in some hints at least of what general level of adventurism the group contemplates.

Letters home often show the signs of mounting panic or suspiciousness that presage an individual's breakdown or a group's dangerous acting out. David Dubow's alarming symptoms would certainly have become known if he had been exchanging letters with his family. The paranoid tenor of mail from people in Jonestown prior to their suicide should not have been hard to interpret. Since one can't control the state of mind that makes these young people vulnerable to catastrophe, it is parents' responsibility to keep the lines of communication open at least, so they may be warned of danger.

Developments such as deterioration of a member's physical or mental health, his endangerment from terrorist activities or from a leader's paranoid hysteria may well warrant the person's removal from his group—but there is no easy way to do it. The law in some jurisdictions allows parents to seek conservatorship of their child by court order for a "cooling-off" period of thirty or sixty days. With such an order, a member can be forcibly removed from the group. To obtain conservatorship, it must be demonstrated to the court's satisfaction that the remedy is a "lesser evil" than what might otherwise occur. There are other restrictions too, although they vary from area to area. For example, one might have to prove mental incompetence to show that the child is incapable of making a wise decision in his own behalf, or demonstrate that his staying is not under his own volition. Such restrictions can seldom be met, and conservatorships are rarely granted to parents of radical departers. The state of California, in 1977, revoked conservatorship altogether on the basis that it was unconstitutional.

Conservatorship is restrictive for good reason. If it were not, parents could meddle in the lives of even their grown-up children whenever they disapproved of their voluntary choices. What might merely seem an experiment in living to one family might seem to be a radical departure to another, and fundamental rights of the child would be impossible to protect.

Were a family to succeed in getting their child home for a month or two during the height of commitment, he might be spared tragedy within the group if it is imminent. However, there is little chance that he will be swayed from his beliefs or be prevented from rejoining his group at the end of that time. Conservatorship is not imprisonment; the child can't be prevented from coming and going as he pleases, from being in the company of fellow members, or, indeed, of practicing his faith just as he did within the group. Unless a person is shown to be a danger to himself or others—that is, suicidal or violent—commitment to a mental hospital is entirely voluntary, even with obvious symptoms of psychosis.

As when the young person was within the group, persuasion by reason or emotional plea meets with impenetrability. Therapy also is ineffectual at this point, since the joiner is not ready to exercise insight. Until the joiner himself has completed the internal reorganization that is the prelude to doubting the group and rapprochement with the family, he will have "returned" in a technical sense only.

Frustrated by both the limitations of the law and their child's impenetrability, thousands of parents have resorted to kidnapping and deprograming. Both are illegal. Children have brought suit against their families and deprogramers, and have also entered class actions on behalf of their group. Most such suits have been found in favor of the complainants. Kidnapping is kidnapping even when a parent does it in what he or she believes to be the best interests of the child. Forcible restraint, as when Ethan was locked into that lakeside bungalow for seventy-two hours, is just as clearly against the law and has been judged so by the courts.

Be that as it may—and there are communities in which police and courts look the other way when kidnapping and deprograming occur, and many cases in which no complaint is made—the welfare of the child is not served by duplicity and duress. I cannot say strongly enough how destructive I have found deprograming at the height of a child's commitment to be, whether, as in Ethan's case, it fails or whether it "works."

Most of the time deprograming does not work. More accurately, it works against the possibility that the joiner will resolve his conflicts, leave the group, and rejoin his family in the mature and loving relationship that cements generation to generation.

Ethan Browning surfaced from the Hare Krishna in 1983, seven years from the start of his radical departure. He was by then 23 years old, the age at which most children have graduated from college. He does not have even a high-school diploma. He had not spoken to his parents for six years. Indeed, they had not seen his face since the day after his deprograming at the age of 16, and when a meeting was arranged after his return, they didn't easily recognize in this tall young man the slip of a boy they had once known.

Relations between the Brownings and Ethan are cordial, but it is doubtful whether they will ever warm with the nostalgia that is the very breath of a family. The scents of Christmas morning and the surprise of childhood toys put away for the grandchildren to one day discover may not be enough to leap a gap of seven years of estrangement. The Browning family album stops abruptly at the moment of Ethan's departure.

All through those years, deprograming prevented the usual rhythm of a radical departure. Ethan had doubts at many times during his stay. He considered leaving. But, each time, his recollection of the kidnapping and deprograming reared up as a barrier to his return. He saw no one beyond that wall to whom he might safely go. Inside the group were men willing to stand beside him as a father might have done, and to these men he gave the filial devotion his own father might have enjoyed.

Even after leaving the Hare Krishna, Ethan has maintained a strong sense of his bond with them. He lives in Newport, Rhode Island, with a friend who is himself a former member of the Hare Krishna. Their diet and their practice of meditation have not changed. Together they share the years of memories to which the Brownings can never gain access.

That is not the only loss. Ethan, so gifted and with so natural a bent for inquiry, works in a waterfront shop selling boating equipment. Although he is content and has renewed his old interest in sailing, this is only a crumb of the banquet of promise he seemed to offer. Maybe he will go on from there; maybe he won't. Just now, he is society's loss as well as his family's.

When deprograming works, the loss is even greater. Halted in their radical endeavor before they have been able to utuilize the group self in their own behalf, former members are thrown back upon just the psychological dependency on parents they had attempted to break away from. The more the parents have achieved their purpose—that is, the more children now realize their "mistake"—the less former members trust their own ability to make wise choices and the more dangerous it seems to them to do anything on their own. In other words, they find it all the more difficult to grow up.

Like other reformed "sinners," successfully deprogramed former members feel great hostility toward the group they once found congenial and now preach against it with the same fervor with which they once proselytized for it. Such "success stories" may join the ranks of obsessive anticult vigilantes and often themselves become deprogramers. When they do either, they exhibit exactly the alarming traits of intolerance, rigidity, fervent singleness of purpose, and close-minded hostility that are so disturbing during the original commitment. This is a cruel irony, and cannot be what parents intend.

If existing legislation doesn't serve the purpose of extricating young people from seemingly dangerous group membership, and if vigilante methods also don't work out well, couldn't new legislation be formulated that would safeguard children from excesses of abuse during their stay within the group? Better yet, couldn't all these groups simply be legislated out of existence?

Let me take the seemingly more difficult question first: Why not a law outlawing cults? The simple answer is that it offends Western society's way of life and destroys the very basis of freedoms it holds most dear. Its members have dared to entitle each individual to his own beliefs. They have the right to be dogmatic or intolerant, to peddle disgusting, poisonous, or just plain foolish ideas so long as no law is broken in the process. This is true even if the majority were to agree that one or another belief is inimical to society's interests. The right to believe what one will explicitly protects the individual from the majority. If that principle were to be abrogated in one case, it would be abrogated in all cases. One can abhor another's belief, but to sever a person from it is to open everyone to severance from his or her respective faith.

As far as curbing excesses is concerned, present legislation is adequate. Criminal behavior by a group or its leader is no different from criminal behavior within society at large and is equally liable to prosecution. Extortion, theft, tax evasion, illegal restraint, child abuse, prostitution, rape, murder, and terrorism within radical groups must be rooted out, just as they must be from every segment of society. Cults have no particular corner of the criminal market. They have invented no new crimes for which novel legislation is required.

Many people will not agree with me; they feel that a new crime has been invented. Common sense tells people that kids would not throw up all the advantages that money can buy for shabby communes and doubtful causes unless emotional duress were involved. Brainwashing was successfully used as a defense in the Patty Hearst trial. Other former members who have turned against their groups support the assumption that their former compliance was forced by their reports of various techniques of group pressure, such as isolation during a retreat, deprivation of privacy at almost all times, exhausting daily regimes, with loss of sleep and stringent diet, and the hyperstimulation of barrages of lecturing and exhortation.

However, the facts don't support an assumption of duress either during recruitment or for the length of their stay. Going back to the very beginning of a radical departure, when the first approach is made, the visit offered, the invitation to a retreat extended, one sees that the percentage of potential joiners who drop out at each escalation of group pressure also escalates, so that of every 250 youngsters in a critical period who are approached, only one or two actually join the group. If recruitment techniques are so sinister as to constitute a hazard to a child's common sense, why do they so rarely work? The answer, of course, is that few children are looking for what radical groups have to offer. They don't buy it because they don't want it. Those who do, usually get what they wanted.

The voluntary nature of a radical departure is crucial to understanding the phenomenon at all, and therefore to knowing what to do about it. When Suzanne Marquette told her mother that no one was doing anything to her, she was telling the truth. The experience of a radical departure is not a passive one. The joiner actively seeks circumstances in which he will feel comfortable and a state of mind that will free him from conflict. He elicits and engages the group's protection from the moment that he lingers, catches an eye, makes a remark. Given the chance to divest himself of material goods, he does so gratefully. Offered the opportunity to abdicate responsibility, he is relieved. Allowed to efface his personal self, he hastens to give it up. Presented with others to adulate, he embraces them with all the passion of a frightened child reunited with the parents he has strayed from.

This doesn't mean that radical groups are innocent of using group-pressure techniques to assure conformity. They do. So too do businesses intent on whipping up the enthusiasm of their sales forces, preachers who seek generous donations from their congregations, politicians who depend on fervent solidarity from their volunteer work forces, football teams who require cheering support. Scenarios for inspiring intense involvement are permanent aspects of the human comedy. They have resulted in the malevolence of Hitler's dictatorship. And perhaps a similar vulnerability to hope when a leader can work his magic inspired the heady days of President John F. Kennedy's ascendancy in Camelot. The psychology of commitment had best be judged by its outcome and not by its means.

The short-term outcome of a young person's recruitment into the group is not likable. Some psychiatrists consider the characteristic array of symptoms, from tunnel vision to uncontagious bliss, to be a pathological syndrome. Others argue that this is not the "real" person, as though the actual child had been replaced with an artificial dummy. Psychiatry can make neither judgment. Mourning, for example, takes extreme forms in many societies but it would be inaccurate to call this necessary time of psychic reorganization pathological however it is expressed. Concepts of authenticity and spuriousness are in the realm of perception, not fact. The real child parents think they know is what the joiner himself perceives to be spurious; when he himself feels genuine within the group, others see his expressions as artificial. One can't argue the reality of feelings; they are what they feel like.

Indeed, the realness of a new joiner's happiness is such that, once committed, wild horses couldn't drag him from his commune. But in commitment, as in recruitment, many people assume coercion. It seems to them impossible that a well-rounded fellow like Philip Holtzman could be transformed within weeks into a bigot with a benign smile unless duplicity had been practiced on him. I would say *complicity* is the accurate word.

The group can bear to express itself, both lovingly and hostilely, only with the tacit understanding that no individual will be called upon either to love or to hate all by himself. That's an example of exquisite mutuality; no one has been duped. There is as much complicity between the leader and his membership as there is among members themselves. The leader doesn't have to crank himself up like the Wizard of Oz; the membership does that for him so long as he doesn't spoil the illusion by stepping from behind his curtain. The best-kept secret of all in this incredible mutuality is the mutual exploitation on which it is based and which is revealed to all parties only on the occasion of a member leaving the group. Then, and only then, the departing member feels that he has been deceived, the other members feel that they have been betrayed, and the leader feels exposed. Until that time all the players have enjoyed a beneficial complicity, each to his own personal gain.

When one can admit to the underlying psychology of a radical departure, there is no one left to blame except oneself. Parents always ask me that agonized question "Where have *we* gone wrong?" I don't think parents have gone wrong in any specific or personal way for which they should assume guilt.

As members of the middle class, the families of radical departers have raised their children to be successful in that context. They have tried to foster individualism and self-reliance. They have introduced a relativistic value system in which broad tolerance—but also expediency—is required. For middle-class purposes, a person who put communality above self-interest and absolutism above relativism would be at a disadvantage.

Until the modern era, in Western nations, just the opposite was true. Almost all cultures relied on communality among their members and assured it with an absolute belief system. In such a society, individualism was considered aberrant and was frowned upon. Broad appreciation of varying perspectives threatened the community's cementing belief and was frequently repressed or obliterated.

Human development is rather flexible, and adolescents in general show a readiness to fit in with either of these cultural extremes. Yet not all people are alike. Young people's development follows a course that to some extent is dictated by their own internal needs and timetables as well as by their very private experience of relationship within their families. Radical departers seem to be individuals who by their nature and their emotional experience are readier to fit in with a communal and absolutist social structure than an individualistic and relativistic one. That is neither their fault nor that of their parents.

Nor do I think it productive to rail against society. For better or for worse, hopes have been placed in the strength of pluralism and in the progress and creativity of individualism. Whatever resolutions may be discovered to help children who find these choices difficult to grow up with will have to be sought within the framework of the culture and institutions society values.

The best possible resolution would be to forestall radical departures before the unhappy accident of an approach takes place, and cure what ails the child by other means.

The prospect of deterring a young person from a radical departure is not bright. There is the problem of recognition. Expecting adolescents to go through ups and down, parents ignore warning signals. Thinking evenness to be equivalent to adjustment, they aren't alarmed by lack of progress. The young person himself is therefore in a "damned if I do, damned if I don't" situation. He fails in his attempt to signal his distress by acting up, like Fred or Nancy. As with Phil and Dennis, compliance fails to make clear his stalemate either.

As a psychiatrist, I would caution all parents to take seriously any prolonged period of lack of progress toward what constitutes maturation in today's society. They should be concerned, and they should express their concern out loud to their sons and daughters.

For some years, I've written a twice-weekly newspaper column to answer letters received from adolescents and young adults. Over and over again, those who write with painful uncertainties confide that they have told no one of their problem. If children are so reluctant to admit their pain, perhaps parents must take the first step. Some open the door to communication by mentioning problems they had at that time in their own lives, or admitting to uncertainties or pain they feel in the present. Others worry aloud about what they have observed of their child's distress, and suggest that there might be some relief in talking about it. There's no guarantee that openness will become reciprocal, but at least the offer has been tendered.

What to do even then, however, remains problematical. If Dennis had confided his sense of spuriousness, how might that have helped the Ericsons make up their own minds about the draft? Should they have participated in his draft-dodging; marched him off to the nearest army recruitment office even before the draft notice arrived? If the Lewises could have discovered that Nancy was quite unsure of her dramatic talents, should they have called her cards or supported her bluff? I think these problems go deeper than last-ditch efforts can reach.

Even without knowing joiners' very early experience of their relationship with parents, I would hazard a guess that their dependency has deep roots. I notice that joiners' parents are perhaps more willing than most to participate intimately in their children's lives, by, for example, prolonged financial support, decision-making, or undemandingness. But I as easily notice that these children elicit support and make little effort to differentiate themselves. Parents give them what they ask for. These patterns are longstanding and cannot be changed on short notice.

Mental health professionals are the first to suggest therapy as a cure for stalemated relationships, but therapy isn't something one can do either for or to someone. Like a radical departure, therapy is a voluntary joining from which the joiner derives strength to get his own internal work accomplished. For all the reasons given earlier, potential joiners in their critical period are unwilling to present themselves for probing and unlikely to be able to utilize the therapeutic situation for insight. Unable to exercise prevention, parents may have to let these children go.

But not necessarily into the Moonies.

If these children so particularly need commitment and communality that is at variance with how their parents live, society can provide it. There are prototypes for acceptable radical departures in many countries.

Canada's Katimavik program for youth is federally sponsored. Young men and women over 18 and with a high-school diploma may volunteer for one year's service to their country in construction, environmental, or social-care projects. They work on Indian reservations, in wilderness areas, and in urban slums. As with radical groups, Katimavik members live communally and simply under a leader's care. Leaders themselves tend to be youthful idealists. Members experience belief and belonging quite similar to what radical departers find. Their self-esteem rises as they know themselves to be useful to others and able to care for themselves within the group. There is a new focus for their hopes about the future and the part they might play in safeguarding it. For that year, they find a home away from home—and away from the many choices, pressures, and conflicts that may have seemed insurmountable obstacles to them.

A measure of how well Katimavik serves the middle class is that it is always oversubscribed. Other countries that have provided opportunities for youth's passionate idealism and hope of community have had a similar experience. The London-based Commonwealth Youth Corps sends young people from all over the Commonwealth to its affiliated countries for similar socially oriented projects. It too has fewer places than applicants.

The United States put its best foot forward with VISTA and the Peace Corps during the early 1960s. VISTA sent young volunteers to lend a helping hand in all sorts of rural and urban projects, from setting up a cottage industry among Alabama quilters living below the poverty level, to tutoring children in Harlem. Peace Corps members were sent on missions in other countries to teach construction and other self-help skills. Although technically still alive, both programs can be considered moribund for the purpose of providing an alternative to those vulnerable to radical departure. The Peace Corps now accepts only older men and women, preferably married couples, who have advanced skills to offer. Pathetically, VISTA now supports a membership of 600 youngsters. There is cause for optimism, however. Former governor Jerry Brown established the California Conservation Corps to enable youth to work on socially useful projects, and New York City's Mayor Ed Koch supports the idea of a national youth corps. Such projects not only alleviate youth unemployment but facilitate the developmental and ideological tasks of our young people.

So far, national programs reach too few. Sensing the generality of adolescent yearnings for belief and belonging, some have suggested a universal youth corps, federally funded and compulsory. There are pitfalls in any compulsory program that is run by government bureaucracy and involves tens of thousands of youth from every sort of background. Would inspiration be lost in institutionalism? Could such a program screen out, as the armed services do, those who aren't physically or emotionally prepared to live with the demands of discipline and hard work? If so, what does it mean to tell teen-agers they are not good enough to serve society?

It would take many years of public debate to explore the feasibility of so broad an innovation, but it would be worth it if only to awaken everyone to the dimensions of the dilemma faced by children. If people are willing to discuss openly the difficulties in the value system that are implicated in radical departure, I think they could find many choices more appropriate than compulsory service in a pluralistic society. Notice that programs now serving youth are perhaps too similar to "the system" to help vulnerable individuals. Scouting, for example, has traditionally reflected self-centered values—competition, merit awards, and product—although recently community action programs have been emphasized.

Neighborhoods, towns, churches, and temples might consider service-oriented programs in which cooperation replaces competition and contribution replaces product. Businesses might think of donating money; and municipalities could set aside acreage for camps. Surely everyone can think of work to be done in their own communities and in others'.

A greater variety of service programs, personally inspired, directed toward heartfelt community goals, and enrolling small numbers of youth, would nicely complement voluntary service on a national basis. Small programs could range from eight-week summer camps, to urban communes dedicated to environmental or renovation tasks, to one- or two-year programs as a temporary alternative to college, or even in coordination with universities willing to advance credit for "hands-on" education.

To do this, it would be necessary to put aside fear of radical groups and learn from them. What are their economics, optimal group size, living arrangements? What are the tasks and how are they apportioned? How do they structure discipline; what is accomplished in group meetings; how important is the role of rituals, songs, and other communal activities? It will not do to subvert radical-group values in an attempt to make them better match society's; that is just what has gone wrong as far as youth is concerned.

Knowing what is now known about radical departures, one might be concerned that society's approval of a group is itself a subversion of members' need to rebel. The joiners looked at here purposefully chose groups that, in their parents' perception especially, represented antagonism to family and society. How can they break away if parents give them their blessing?

Remember, however, that by the time these young men and women were offered the opportunity to break away, they had suffered a prolonged period of decreasing self-esteem and mounting desperation. Also, their pain was not acknowledged, often barely guessed, by friends, family, or the rest of the adult world. I think general acknowledgment that adolescent aspirations differ in kind and in degree from adult goals would go a long way toward alleviating the loneliness radical departers experience. I also believe that were ease for their pain to be offered earlier, their breaking away need not be so violent. Rebellion, as I emphasized earlier, isn't necessarily accompanied by hostility and is usually benign. A joining that was exclusive to youth, antimaterialistic, and intended to repair some of the damage the adult world has wrought offers sufficient smugness. Leaving home for a while in token opposition to parents' hopes that their child will continue smoothly from high school through college offers enough defiance. In fact, the armed services have provided radical departure to youth from families that had pinned their hopes elsewhere. I think one can afford to endure a modicum of adolescent smugness and defiance in children's ultimate interest.

Can *they* afford one or two years' respite from the rat race? The Mormon church, whose youthful members are rarely seen among the ranks of radical departers, encourages eighteen months' missionary or social service from members in this age group, and a very large number accept the challenge. The Mormons are among the most prosperous, well-educated, and successful middle-class groups in our society. Eighteen months of youthful service doesn't seem to dent their progress toward careers.

Most reassuring of all, radical departers themselves progress into middle-class adulthood in a way that seems nearly indistinguishable from the progress of their contemporaries.

Radical departers don't go back to being exactly the same sort of person they were before they left. Frequently there is a shift of interest, sometimes necessitated by the time lost from career training, but also related to genuinely spiritual or charitable aspirations experienced within the group.

Jennifer Green wasn't able to make up for lost time in her piano training and no longer felt comfortable with the degree of self-involvement so demanding a career would have required. Upon her graduation from college with a double major, in music and psychology, she got a job working in a nursery school for emotionally disturbed children. The serendipitous double major seemed to fall into place: the children, she found, could use music to help themselves become organized and as a bridge to communication with others. She became particularly interested in one severely ill child, an autistic boy who was unable to use language in a communicative way and who shied from every sort of human contact. Using the piano, each of them separately at first, she was able to help this boy "make music" with another human, and his progress stirred her.

Jennifer had turned thirty the last time I spoke with her. She had by then completed a degree in special education and, with her parents' financial help, had just opened her own small school for emotionally disturbed children. I asked her how she felt now about her year at the Healing Workshop. At first, she answered offhandedly that she had been a kid then, after all. But then she reconsidered. Perhaps their techniques had been nonsense, but what she had striven for then she was achieving now: a reaching out to others, a higher level of interaction. She chose not to emphasize that she is also a competant and self-reliant person, but of course she is.

Philip Holtzman maintained conscious bonds with Orthodoxy as he continued through college. When I called him, he had turned 26 and was in his first year at medical school. After some vacillation about what degree of Orthodoxy he felt comfortable with, he came to the conclusion that the Jewish identity that had been such a revelation to him while at the yeshiva could not be put aside. He had donned the skullcap again, though he wears no side locks, and conducts his life in as close an approximation of Orthodoxy as is possible for a person functioning outside the Orthodox community. He corresponds regularly with his closest friend in the yeshiva, who is now studying to become a rabbi, and hopes to go back to Israel for his medical residency one day. He has thought of the possibility of living there permanently.

Phil's depth of seriousness has had an effect on his parents too. Although they remain Reform Jews, preparing kosher meals only when Phil visits, Dr. Holtzman feels less conflicted about the disparity between his upbringing and his present observance. The beautiful candle-lighting ceremony performed at sundown on Fridays to mark the beginning of the Sabbath within the home is now an integral part of the Holtzman family's life. It seems to me both generations have gained.

I have found it reassuring that even former members who had a particularly trying time upon their return can recover fully. Nancy Lewis Carson has been able to maintain the gains she made through her membership in the Children of God and afterward in the therapy she required. While completing the commercial course at junior college, she met Alan Carson, then a dentistry student at Rutgers and a friend of that favorite cousin, Becky, whose visit had sparked Nancy's return. They were married within the year. At this time, Alan's practice allows the Carsons a comfortable life without the overtones of financial worry that had caused pressure in Nancy's own family during her childhood. This has allowed her flamboyance an expression that is more in keeping with her actual talents than her theatrical pretensions had been. Her home and her clothing are styled with a merry flair, full of color and texture. At the moment, she is busy with twin daughters, but she takes courses that will eventually lead to a degree in interior design.

"And what became of Sarah Bernhardt?" I wondered aloud. Nancy laughed. She had played the part of Tzeitle, the flamboyantly impulsive daughter in *Fiddler on the Roof*, in a community-center production recently. "I wasn't Sarah Bernhardt," she admitted, "but I was damn good!"

There is a common belief that former members, upon their return, vilify the groups to which they belonged and look back upon that period of their lives with shock and distaste. As has been noted, this is true for many members who have been forced to leave their group before they could choose to do so on their own. It is rarely true of those who have left voluntarily. Almost always, they are able to extract from their experience permanent values which they do their best to integrate into their present lives. Sometimes it is a matter of separating good ends from bad means, as Fred Vitelli had to do when he left the Armed Guard. At other times, it is more a matter of separating the wheat from the chaff—aspects of nonsense or strangeness from underlying values. Suzanne Marquette, for example, had to separate Moonie peculiarities from the underlying faith that had been so sustaining during her membership. That faith is still strong. Eight years after her departure, she attends church regularly and teaches Sunday school.

Suzanne is now Mrs. George Judd, a social worker, mother, housewife, skating coach, and community activist—a lot for a woman still in her mid-twenties. The enthusiastic altruism she enjoyed while with the Moonies has not deserted her at all. She had at first thought her professional work should be among adolescents—the wide-eyed innocents she had enjoyed working with during her departure—but with the birth of her son that schedule became too demanding, and she now works part-time at a geriatric center reminiscent of the nursing home at which she had done volunteer work during her high-school days. She teaches ice-skating weekend afternoons, when her husband, a corporation lawyer, enjoys spending time alone with their one-year-old. Through her church, she organizes community self-help programs in the poorer neighborhoods of the parish. She is still effusive, and her infectious charm goes a long way toward convincing others to donate money, materials, apprenticeships, municipal funds. She thinks anything is possible if you try!

Since this busyness and energy had been permanent aspects of her personality before her radical departure, during it, and since her return, I asked Suzanne if she could characterize for me how she herself had experienced her busyness during those three periods of her life. She recalled easily the way in which she had used busyness as a defense against feeling that "everything would come crashing down" in the months before her departure. Her recollection of her activities with the Moonies was a happy one, and, she felt, they had not been a waste of time, although now she was surprised that the extent of her interests had been so narrow then. As for the present, she reported that she is feeling "terrific" about herself, her family, and her work. "There is nothing I'm doing now that I don't enjoy," she told me, with an intensity of pleasure that was, now, entirely contagious.

I am always impressed with the way in which these young men and women can use and reuse aspects of their personalities for different purposes at different stages of their development. It's not even necessary that an aspect of personality be "good" in order for it to be put ultimately to good service and to give pleasure. Fred Vitelli had bar-

ricaded himself with anger, and, although there's no doubt that criticizing others may feel better than suffering from one's own vulnerability
to criticism, he had carried the chip on his shoulder without enjoy-
ment.

He had been home from his radical departure into the Armed Guard
for only a little over two years when I last spoke with him, but already
I could see he was finding a good use for "bad" anger. He had enrolled in college with a major in political science. Along the walls of
the tiny studio apartment he had fashioned for himself over his parents' garage, I noticed many volumes of history, politics, and law.
During the summer and as part-time work when he can fit it in, he is
a paraprofessional for a legal aid society. He intends to continue on to
law school.

He started to tell me of the latest injustices he had become involved in. His voice rose in anger. I was delighted. There is injustice,
there are things to criticize, and an angry young man like Fred is just
the person to do something about them—as a lawyer, not as a terrorist.

Since the relationship with parents is at the bottom of a radical
departure, I always ask former members how they are getting on with
their parents as the years go by and how they would feel if their own
children one day joined a group similar to the one they joined. They
never wish their own children to go through a radical departure, no
matter how well they have been able to sort out their own experience
and integrate it into their lives. They remain aware that their action
was a desperate one; they hope their children will never experience the
pain that led up to it. If they have become parents, it is also incon-
ceivable to them that their sons or daughters would ever wish for so
abrupt and cruel a breaking away. Most have, however, healed that
wound with their own parents.

Nancy Lewis found that even though there were many things she
really did not share in common with her parents, they were people she
could enjoy being with. All three Lewis sisters now have families of
their own and are settled in at no great distance from their original
northern New Jersey home. They have become one of those families

that like to get the whole tribe together on any occasion that provides the slightest excuse.

Philip Holtzman's and Suzanne Marquette's relationships with their families are uneventfully normal. Fred Vitelli will always be his mother's darling, but he no longer manipulates her devotion. His father shakes his head about this son still. "Always in trouble with the law," he grumbles to his wife, making a joke about Fred's shift from troublemaker to troubleshooter. But Mr. Vitelli's sense that Fred is impractical hasn't stood in the way of a quite pleasant father-son relationship.

Jennifer Green remained unusually close to her mother, and though she is self-supporting now and has her own apartment, she joins her family for Sunday meals every weekend. I asked her about romantic interests; she is even more beautiful as a mature woman than she had been as a girl. She is not ready for a serious relationship, she replied, although she dates occasionally. It may be that she is still working out some of the issues that led to her departure.

Jamie Gould did not manage to find a basis for rapprochement with his father, and has let his mother more or less drift out of his life since her divorce from his father and his own marriage to Julia. Now thirty-two, Jamie has come into his $4-million trust fund, still lives in the house in New York, and still runs the original bookshop he opened after he left the Church of Scientology. In the four years since then, the store has grown to a chain of five bookshops, particularly popular with students. The robust growth of his business is due to his smart marketing and good management, and also to the fact that he did not have to go hat in hand to banks for loans to support expansion. Whenever he saw a choice location, he simply went to his father for no-interest cash. His own trust fund remains intact.

It took rather incessant probing to get these facts from Jamie. He boasted of his success, with good cause, but was reluctant to admit that Mr. Gould had played any part in it. Similarly, he emphasized his ambition to become a millionaire "on my own," although I couldn't see in what way that could come about when the financial backing and risk were really his father's. Still, if such a use of John Gould's money reflects the original longings for dependence that had paralyzed

Jamie before his departure, even that dependency has become more serviceable to him and, I imagine, more gratifying to his father.

One would think that Jamie could more easily identify with his father now that he too is successful in the business world. But again I sensed a lack of resolution in this father-son relationship, since Jamie would say only that his business acumen was learned in the Church of Scientology; he apparently saw no link between his own and his father's similar skills.

Interestingly, Jamie and Julia don't plan to have any children. I don't know enough about Julia's history to guess why she is reluctant to be a mother; she works full time in the business and has been responsible for the striking design of the stores. But I do suppose that Jamie, like others who found little gratification in their own childhood and adolescence, is reluctant to trust himself to parenting.

Kathy O'Connor also was not able to resolve her relationship with her parents. When I last visited with her, she seemed quite at a loss. The Sri Chinmoy, which she had joined after her upsetting disillusion with the Maharaj Ji in the Divine Light Mission, had not proved to be as gratifying as her first radical departure. To outsiders, the group is certainly more appealing. It is less intense, demanding, and ritualistic. Sri Chinmoy activities are more in keeping with contemporary realities and more directed toward concrete projects in the outside world. Far from being paranoid about the "enemy," Sri Chinmoy encourages members to lead a secular life, participating in education, career, and relationships outside the group. Kathy, for example, was prevailed upon to continue in nursing while a member, and did answer an ad that resulted in her becoming a nursing supervisor at a pediatric hospital in Baltimore.

Sri Chinmoy is similar to 3HO in its nice balance between asceticism and worldly involvement, and Dennis Ericson was able to use just that aspect of his group for his own growth. Kathy couldn't. She seemed to have needed the Divine Light Mission's group neurosis in order to avoid suffering neurosis herself. When denied that expression, she couldn't maintain interest in Sri Chinmoy. By the time of our last conversation, when Kathy was in her early thirties and a decade had passed since the time of her first radical departure, she was distressed with her administrative job, had left Sri Chinmoy, felt her friendships were shallow, had no interest in men, and, it seemed clear, was quite depressed.

To combat her sense of "being nowhere" she had joined a Catholic relief agency and enjoyed the volunteer work—in fact that might have pleased the O'Connors had she told them of it. But she hadn't. Speaking of her family, she became more distressed. Her perception was that her parents had written her off. (Years before, she had told me that when her parents disapproved of her relationship with Michael, *she* had written *them* off!) Similarly, she remarked that her former husband, Michael, "would have nothing to do with" her though why he should when he was by that time remarried and the father of three children she could not say. More and more bitter, she brought up again the "betrayal" of the Maharaj Ji; everything in her life had gone against her.

Toward the end of the conversation, Kathy asked me to suggest a therapist, and I did. Perhaps this was a good sign. It may be that she will eventually be able to place her problems in herself, where they properly belong, instead of casting them as evils in the outside world. That is the usual result of a radical departure, and if a youngster must go through one, it is doubly sad when they are unable to utilize it.

I have become particularly fond of Dennis Ericson because I have known him for so long. He was thirty-four in 1983 and still in the 3HO. Fourteen years had passed since he and I, for our separate reasons, had found ourselves involved with the urban commune movement in Canada. The oldest of my own three boys is sixteen now, and I bought for him a *futon* of the kind Dennis still sells in the Japanese mattress stores in Vancouver. His clientele is upper middle class; *futons* have become chic. Dennis has become a businessman. He is a sturdy man; conservative, sensible, and mature. He married Judith, who is also a member of 3HO; together they run two stores and also manage the central accounting for all the Vancouver businesses of their group. They remind me of Mr. and Mrs. Vitelli in a way—self-made, hard-working people who take no shortcuts to success.

Perhaps I can allow myself to muse on Dennis's future since I know him so well. Judith was pregnant the last I know, so there will be a grandchild in the Ericson family soon. I think the birth of the baby will strengthen Dennis's ties with his mother and father, and Judith's ties with her family in Sacramento. There will be more visits back and forth, the old holidays spent together, less exclusive involvement in the group and more involvement with the child's teachers, school friends, and other parents outside the group. And I think Dennis will come out of 3HO.

I have been reassuring throughout this book. I think reassurance will go a long way toward resolving radical departures. I haven't had to force this bedside manner on myself; the facts warrant a sanguine view. Yet I have also hoped to show the abandonment these young men and women feel because family and society fail to meet their needs, and the dangers we court in allowing less responsible or frankly exploitive people to do our job for us.

However lovingly and carefully children are raised, there will always be some who meet obstacles to their growing up. Some will seek a detour that is for them the better path. And, fortunately, many of these sons and daughters will be able to use this detour to arrive at their own vision of success, one that rests in commitment and community, in belief and belonging.

The creative flexibility and richness of today's culture needs Nancy's verve, Dennis's gentleness, Phil's faith, Jennifer's givingness, Fred's sense of justice, and Suzanne's community spirit. They are the benefactors.

When I began my work, outrage was just arousing people to recognition of radical departures. In the years since, that outrage has clouded comprehension. There is no excuse for that any more. Who these children are, why they make their radical departures, and what becomes of them are known. It is time for outrage to subside. There is a job to be done. I think it can be done.

Suggested Reading

Adelson, J., "The Development of Ideology in Adolescents." In *Adolescence in the Life Cycle*, edited by S. Dragastin and G. Elder. New York: John Wiley, 1976.

Braungart, R., "Youth and Social Movements." In *Adolescence in the Life Cycle*, edited by S. Dragastin and G. Elder. New York: John Wiley, 1976.

Bromley, D. G., and A. D. Shupe, Jr., *Strange Gods*. Boston: Beacon Press, 1981.

Cox, H., *Turning East*. New York: Simon & Schuster, 1977.

Galanter, M., "Charismatic Religious Sects and Psychiatry: An Overview." *American Journal of Psychiatry* 139 (1982):1539–1548.

Galanter, M., R. Rabkin, and A. Deutsch, "The 'Moonies': A Psychological Study of Conversion and Membership in a Contemporary Religious Sect." *American Journal of Psychiatry* 136 (1979):165–170.

Greeley, A., *Ecstasy: A Way of Knowing*. Englewood Cliffs, NJ: Prentice-Hall, 1964.

Hedgepeth, W., and D. Stock, *The Alternative: Communal Life in New America*. New York: Macmillan, 1970.

Kanter, R. M., *Commitment and Community: Communes and Utopias in Sociological Perspective*. Cambridge: Harvard University Press, 1972.

Kaslow, F., and M. B. Sussman, *Cults and the Family*. New York: The Haworth Press, 1982.

Keniston, K., *The Uncomitted: Alienated Youth in America*. New York: Harcourt, Brace & World, 1965.

Lande, N., *Mindstyles / Lifestyles*. Los Angeles: Price Stern Sloan, 1976.

Levine, S. V., "Alienated Jewish Youth and Religious Seminaries: An Alternative to Cults?" In *Psychodynamic Perspectives on Religion, Sect and Cult*, edited by David A. Halperin. Boston: John Wright PSG, 1983.

———, "Alienation as an Affect in Adolescents." In *The Adolescent and Mood*

Disturbance, edited by H. Golombek and B. Garfinkel. New York: International Universities Press, 1983.

————, "American Exiles in Canada: A Social and Psychiatric Follow-up." *Psychiatric Opinion* 11 (November 1974): 20–31.

————, "Believing and Belonging." *Adolescent Psychiatry* 7 (1979): 41–53.

————, "Cults and Mental Health: Clinical Conclusions." *Canadian Journal of Psychiatry* 26 (December 1981): 534–539.

————, "The Role of Psychiatry in the Phenomenon of Cults." *Canadian Psychiatric Association Journal* 24 (November 1979): 593–603.

————, Youth and Religious Cults: A Societal and Clinical Dilemma." *Adolescent Psychiatry* 11 (1978): 75–89.

Levine, S. V., and N. Salter, "Youth and Contemporary Religious Movements: A Study of Psychological and Social Implications." *Canadian Psychiatric Association Journal* 21 (1976): 411–420.

McDonald, D., *Cults and the Constitution—A Center Report*. Santa Barbara: Robert Maynard Hutchins Center for the Study of Democratic Institutions, March/April 1982.

Needleman, J., and G. Baker, *Understanding the New Religions*. New York: Seabury Press, 1978.

Prince, R., "Religious Experience, Youth and Social Change." *R. M. Bucke Memorial Society Review* 3 (1968): 1–3.

Rothchild, J., and S. Wolf, *The Children of the Counterculture*. New York: Doubleday, 1976.

Sargant, W., *Battle for the Mind*. New York: Harper & Row, 1971.

Stoner, C., and J. Parke, *All God's Children: The Cult Experience: Salvation or Slavery?* Radnor, PA: Chilton Book, 1977.

West, L. J., and M. T. Singer, "Cults, Quacks, and Nonprofessional Psychotherapies." In *Comprehensive Textbook of Psychiatry III*, 3rd ed., edited by H. I. Kaplan, A. M. Freedman, and B. J. Sadock. Baltimore: Williams and Wilkins, 1980.

Yankelovich, D., *The New Morality: A Profile of American Youth in the 1970's*. New York: McGraw-Hill, 1974.

Zaretsky, I. I., and M. P. Leone, *Religious Movements in Contemporary America*. Princeton: Princeton University Press, 1974.

*Saul V. Levine is Head of the Department of Psychia-
try at Sunnybrook Medical Centre, University of
Toronto, Ontario, and professor of psychiatry at that
university. He received his undergraduate and medical
degrees from McGill University in Montreal, Quebec,
and his psychiatric training at Stanford University in
Palo Alto, California. He is widely published in his
field and in the lay press (he is a regular columnist in a
nationally syndicated advice column to youth in Canada) and serves on a number of international editorial,
advisory, and directorial boards. Dr. Levine is particularly interested in the ideas, people, institutions, and
movements that motivate adolescents and young
adults. His research and teaching in these areas have
been conducted worldwide and have led him to become
aware of the similarities in dilemmas, delights, and
dangers confronting all youth. Although keenly aware
of the enormity of some of the social problems, he
remains an optimist regarding the present and future of
the majority of our young people. He is coauthor of a
book for adolescents entitled* The Answer Book *to be
published in 1986.*

*Dr. Levine lives in Toronto with his wife, Eleanor, a
fitness instructor and geriatric psychiatry social worker,
and three sons, Jaime, 18, Mischa, 16, and Zachary, 12.
He is a keen squash player and skier with a lively
interest in music, chess, hiking, jogging, cuisine, and
politics.*